THE MATHEMATICAL EDGE:
How to put the "+" on your "A"

Essential Performance Skills and Problem-Solving Strategies

THE MATHEMATICAL EDGE:
How to put the "+" on your "A"

Grades 4 through 12

A Resource for Teachers, Homeschoolers, Parents, and Students

James A. Vicich

Come to the edge, He said.
They said, We are afraid.
Come to the edge, He said.
They came.
He pushed them ... and they flew.

–Guillaume Apollinaire

w w w . j a m e s v i c i c h . c o m

Dedication

This book is dedicated to all of the students and teachers with whom I have had the privilege to work alongside, sharing our passion for learning and doing mathematics.

Contents

The Big Picture 1

Part I: Essential Ideas and Productive Problem-Solving Behaviors 3

Part II: Problems for Various Strategies and Essential Content 21

Part III: Learning Tools
(Problem-Solving Templates, and Problem-Solving Performance Flowchart) 77

References 84

Selected Solutions 86

Recommended Resources 103

Additional Answers 104

The Big Picture

For students that possess confidence, a willingness to explore, and productive problem-solving strategies, mathematics can be the key that unlocks many opportunities in life. Sadly, for some students, the study of mathematics becomes an overwhelming challenge that offers little to no guidance for learning productive problem-solving behaviors and performance enhancing tips. This book is written to help all students not only excel but to "put the plus on their A."

The problems I have included in this packet are meant to be challenging yet they provide opportunities to identify, strengthen, and reflect on each aspect of productive problem-solving behaviors.

The most crucial first step in problem solving is to underline the given information and keywords and circle the goal. This is called *initial engagement.*

Next, ask the solver if they can make a reasonable guess (*conjecture*) about the answer (is it a small number say less than 10 or a very large number).

Ask the solver to say aloud what he or she *plans* as the first two or three steps in her/his solution.

Monitoring progress is an important skill. Ask, is what I am doing moving me closer to answer? If not, go back and be sure you know both the given and goal.

Write your answer as a **complete sentence** using precise language, correct grammar, and appropriate units. Avoid saying or simply writing, "10", rather say, "the length of the fence was 10 feet."

Lastly, ALWAYS *verify* (i.e., *check*) that the answer makes sense. Look for more than one solution pathway to arrive at the answer. Convince yourself first, then convince others.

Teachers and parents, please read all of the pages in this book before you start giving problems to your students and children. I love playing golf and golf can be fun but also frustrating at times. Doing mathematics requires a certain state of mind to see math as fun but also to learn to handle the frustration in a productive manner. Persevere, learn from mistakes, have fun, and do not be afraid to stop an unproductive attempt and begin a different path toward the answer. Be sure students label all drawings and press them to explain their thinking aloud. Promote deep, well-connected understandings rather than memorization.

At the beginning of each section, you will find *NOTES TO THE READER*. Please read these notes as if I were speaking to you in person. They give you a road map of the big ideas you will encounter and must master over time to increase your own confidence and competence in doing and teaching mathematics.

Part I
Essential Ideas and Productive Problem-Solving Behaviors
Problem solving is the heart of doing mathematics. –Halmos

Notes to the reader:

Learn the categories of productive problem-solving behavior described in Schoenfeld's Theoretical framework and Finer Grained Description of Problem-Solving Behavior. Encourage students to learn and organize deep, well-connected conceptual understandings as an accessible network/web of ideas. A student's belief system can advance or hinder progress. Create learning experiences that undermine *UNPRODUCTIVE* beliefs (such as there is only one way to solve a problem, usually the teacher's way). Help students learn to deal with frustration. Errors are a natural part of doing mathematics (that is why there is an eraser at the end of every pencil) and should be seen not as failure but as learning opportunities.

The Diagnostic Instrument serves as a checklist for a teacher much like a trauma physician monitors vital signs. Learn to identify each category of a student's problem-solving behavior.

Wanting to share their new understandings of productive problem-solving behaviors, teachers with guidance from Dr. Vicich, created the Problem-Solving Template to help students develop productive habits and to increase students' ability to metacognitively reflect on the quality of their solutions. The templates are extremely useful at the beginning of a semester and as the student becomes proficient can be used periodically to reinforce productive behaviors. The Camera-Ready classroom poster serves to remind students of higher expectations required to put the "+" on the "A."

Problem Solving: What does it mean?

The Definition of a Problem: Three views of what constitutes a mathematical problem are presented in the related literature.

- The definition used by Liljedahl (2021), Schoenfeld (1985), and Kulm (1982) states that a problem is encountered when a specific routine method or algorithm is not known or available to the solver.

- Lester (1977, p. 2) similarly defines a problem as "a situation for which an individual or group is called upon to perform a task for which there is no readily accessible algorithm which determines completely the solution."

- Goldin (1982, p. 97) uses a broader definition that states that "a task is a problem when steps are detected between the posing of the task and the answer."

I prefer to use Goldin's definition of a problem as it allows teachers and students to identify productive behaviors such as identifying givens and goals, making conjectures, planning, strategy selection, monitoring progress, and verification on every task encountered.

Theoretical Framework for Characterizing Problem-Solving Performance

Schoenfeld (1992) outlines a framework for examining what people know, and what they do, as they work on solving problems with substantial mathematical content. Citing a variety of his own research findings and classroom observations, Schoenfeld demonstrates that students' problem-solving performance is not simply the product of what the student knows. Schoenfeld claims that problem-solving performance is also a function of students' perceptions of their knowledge, derived from experiences with mathematics.

Schoenfeld suggests the following framework of knowledge and behavior for characterizing problem-solving performance:

Resources: intuitions, algorithmic procedures, facts, and whatever mathematical information that the student may understand or misunderstand that might bear on a problem;

Heuristics: strategies and techniques for making progress, drawing figures, introducing suitable notation, exploiting related problems, testing and verification procedures;

Control: refers to the way a student uses or fails to use the information at their disposal, planning, monitoring, decision-making, conscious metacognitive acts;

Belief System (One's Mathematical World View): about self, about the topic, about mathematics, about the environment, determines the ways that the knowledge in the first three categories is used.

Writing about the importance of one's belief system, Schoenfeld says that one's beliefs about mathematics can determine how one chooses to approach a problem, which techniques will be used or avoided, and how long and how hard one will work on a problem (Schoenfeld, 1992).

*Good questions to ask yourself during problem solving:
1. What are you doing?
2. Why are you doing it?
3. How will it help you move closer to an answer?
4. Does your answer make sense? Is it reasonable?

Adapted from: Schoenfeld, A.H. (1987). In Cognitive science and mathematics education, What's all the fuss about metacognition? Ed. Schoenfeld, A.H. (Erlbaum, Hillsdale, NJ), pp 189–215.

Using Cognitive Networks to Describe Resource Knowledge

Resource knowledge refers to the knowledge a problem solver brings to the task. The collection of a student's mathematical understandings can be represented by an internal network (Hiebert & Carpenter, 1992). If a network is a deep and narrow vertical hierarchy the breadth of understandings may be limited (e.g., very good in only algebra). If a student tries to memorize ideas without trying to make sense of them he/she runs the risk of losing knowledge when the memory fades because those ideas are not linked as depicted in Sfard's (1991) "mother with too many sons" model. The optimum network may be thought of as a web showing multiple links allowing one to identify similarities and differences between ideas (Hiebert and Carpenter, 1992, p. 67). For the web model, an instructional goal is to help students build a coherent mental network in which all pieces are joined to others with multiple links. The degree of understanding is determined by the number and strength of the connections that a student is able to make within her/his network. The advantage of a web/network is that if one understanding is weak it can be reconstructed or strengthened by the links to other understandings in the web.

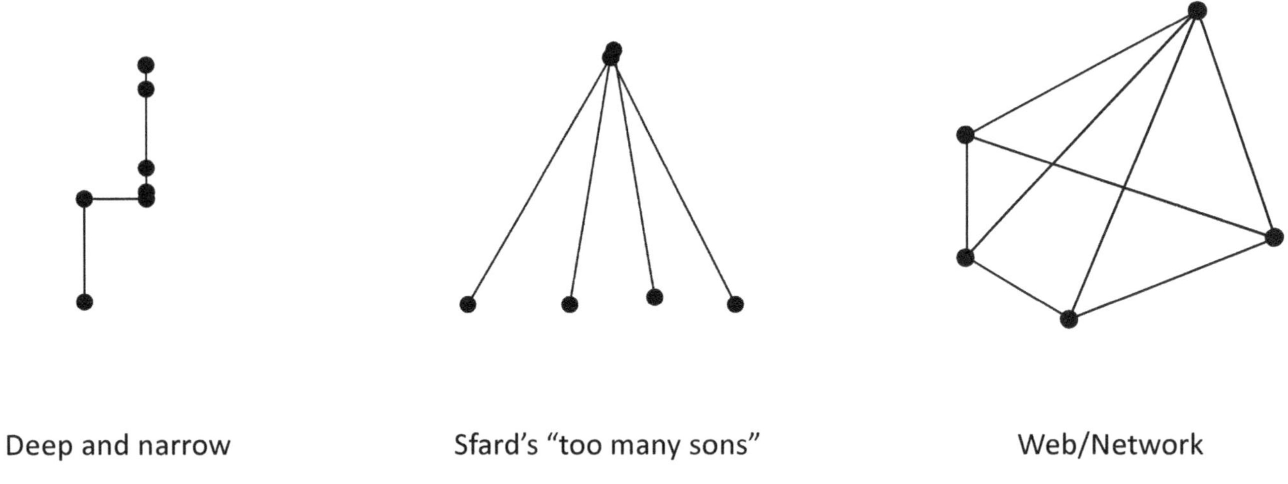

Deep and narrow   Sfard's "too many sons"   Web/Network

Hiebert, J., & Carpenter, T. P. (1992). Learning and teaching with understanding. In D. A. Grouws (Ed.), *Handbook of research on mathematics teaching and learning* (pp. 65-97). New York: McMillan.

Sfard, A. (1991). On the dual nature of mathematical conceptions: reflections on processes and objects as different sides of the same coin. *Educational Studies in Mathematics*, 22, 1-36.

Vicich, J. (2002). *Mathematical Problem-Solving Behaviors of Undergraduate Developmental Algebra Students*. Unpublished doctoral dissertation, Arizona State University, Tempe, AZ.

Finer Grained Description of Problem-Solving Behavior

Orientation/Initial Engagement
- "A well-formed representation allows the student to operate at a level approaching expert performance." (Geiger & Galbraith, 1998, p. 547).
- "Effort is put forth to read and understand the problem. Information is organized. Goals and givens are established and represented. (Carlson & Bloom, 2005, p. 51)

Executive Behaviors
- Planning and Monitoring (Establish Subgoals)
- Selection of Heuristic Strategies
- Verification: "Verification processes are used to validate a solution or part of a solution of a problem (or subgoal) where a problem solver's sense making facility plays a key role in assessing the 'reasonableness' of the outcome in terms of the context. (Geiger & Galbraith, 1998, p. 545)

Resource Knowledge
- Formal and Informal knowledge about the content domain, including facts, definitions, algorithmic procedures, routine procedures, and relevant competencies about the rules of discourse. (Carlson & Bloom, 2005, p. 48)
- "...even when an individual appears to possess the resources to solve a particular problem, they often do not access those resources in the context of producing a problem solution." (p. 48)
- The ability to recall having solved a similar problem may inform a problem solver's behavior. (Source: DeFranco, T. C. (1996). A perspective on mathematical problem-solving expertise based on the performances of male Ph.D. mathematicians. *CBMS Issues in Mathematics Education, 6,* 195 – 213. Providence, RI: American Mathematical Society.

Belief System
- One's beliefs about mathematics can determine how one chooses to approach a problem, which techniques will be used or avoided, and how long and how hard one will work on a problem (Source: Schoenfeld, A. (1992). Unproductive beliefs can cause a solver to give up or not make progress.

Common Unproductive Beliefs Held by Students*

1) Experts move directly from the problem statement to the solution.

2) There is only one way to solve a math problem (usually the teacher's way).

3) It is **not** OK to stop and start overusing a different approach once I've started.

4) I just need to get an answer; it does not have to make sense to me.

5) If I cannot solve a problem in 5 minutes or less then I cannot solve it at all.

6) The best way to learn math is to memorize.

7) Every problem uses a formula to arrive at an answer.

8) Making unsuccessful solution attempts is **not** a natural part of doing mathematics.

* All of these beliefs are counterproductive and are **not** held by expert mathematicians.

Vicich, J. (2002). *Mathematical Problem-Solving Behaviors of Undergraduate Developmental Algebra Students.* Unpublished doctoral dissertation, Arizona State University, Tempe, AZ.
Vicich, J. (2007). Conceptual understanding, problem-solving, communication and assessment meet at the board. *Mathematics Teacher, 100*(6), 420-425.

Carlson, M. (1999). The mathematical behavior of six successful mathematics graduate students: Influences leading to mathematics success. *Educational Studies in Mathematics, 40*, 237 – 258.

Carlson, M. (2000). A study of the mathematical behaviors of mathematicians: The role of metacognition and mathematical intimacy in solving problems. In T. Nakahara & M. Koyama Eds.), *Proceedings of the Twenty-fourth Annual Meeting of the International Group for the Psychology of Mathematics Education, Vol. 2*, (pp. 137 – 144). Hiroshima, Japan. (ERIC Document Reproduction Service No. ED452032

Problem Solving: A State of Mind

Adapting elements of sports psychology and research findings of expert mathematicians' attitudes towards problem solving can be effective in dealing with frustration and building confidence and joy in doing mathematics. Adapted from Rotella, 2008; Carlson, 1999, 2000; Carlson & Bloom, 2005.

- Everyone can "get it" at their own level.
- First, convince yourself that you have "talent" and therefore have a good attitude toward doing mathematics.
- When things get difficult: Rely on fundamentals such as re-establishing the givens and goals; finding patterns; exploring special conditions/cases; draw to help visualize; seek alternative solution paths; always, always, verify that an answer makes sense and is reasonable.
- The more you practice, the better you become.
- Have "fun" with problem solving. Experience the enjoyment of doing math.
- Relax, keep a quiet mind. The rhythm and flow of ideas comes from a quiet mind having fun.
- Learn to handle mistakes.
- Accept that in problem solving mistakes happen, it is a natural part of doing mathematics.
- Use precise language to describe special conditions and cases. Ex.: The *consecutive* numbering of students began with an *even whole* number and ended with an *odd whole* number.
- Every problem **begins** with identifying the *givens* and the *goals*, so underline them. You may need to read the problem several times to achieve clarity.
- Every problem **ends** with *verification* that the answer makes sense and meets the goals of the problem.
- Have a "routine" for solving any problem:
    - Underline the givens and goals.
    - Write a legend for variables/symbols.
    - Draw a picture or make an organized table/chart.
    - Mentally choose from a variety of strategy options.
    - Make a plan: Visualize a solution pathway.
    - Execute your plan, and monitor your progress "Am I moving toward an answer?"
    - Verify answer makes sense.
    - Find an alternative solution pathway that reaches the same answer.
- Practice the routine you will need when under pressure.
- Focus on the "process" of problem solving and the results will follow.

Introducing the Diagnostic Instrument

My long history of working with middle and secondary mathematics teachers reveals that many teachers have (a) limited understanding of productive problem-solving behaviors (most often a variation of Polya's (1981) four-step process: Understand the problem; Devise a plan; Carry out the plan; Look back.), (b) limited awareness of unproductive beliefs, and (c) limited knowledge of problem-solving strategies and heuristics.

As a means of enabling teachers to identify productive problem-solving behaviors, teachers should act as a researcher observing/listening to another's problem-solving behaviors by using the Diagnostic Instrument on the following page. In this protocol solvers are asked to think aloud while observers identify evidence of the various categories of behavior such as initial engagement, planning, conjecturing, strategy selection, monitoring of progress, verification, resource knowledge, as well as beliefs and attitudes such as willingness to explore and persevere.

Teacher behaviors should promote, support, and establish expectations for student behaviors/ actions (adapted from AMP Sustainability Factors available at Strom et al., 2012). These expectations include that (a) students will be engaged in mathematical discourse with the teacher and with fellow students, (b) students will be explaining their mathematical thinking, (c) students will be justifying their reasoning mathematically, (d) students will critique the thinking of others, (e) mathematical reasoning will be the ultimate authority to determine the validity of a claim and students will need to convince their own classmates through sound and logical reasoning, (f) students will be engaged in problem-solving, (g) students will be communicating (verbally and in writing) mathematical thinking coherently and precisely (language), (h) students will be sharing alternative solution pathways, and (i) students will embrace mistakes and remain persistent when problem solving.

Diagnostic Instrument for Problem-Solving Behaviors
(Vicich, 2020, Adapted from Geiger & Galbraith, 1998)

Engagement

Problem is read	Key words underlined	Givens and goals established	Givens and goals represented symbolically

*Executive Behaviors

*Planning: Did you make a *plan* or "jump into" this problem? Did you make any *conjectures regarding the answer or possible solution path*?

*Monitoring/Control

Recognition that a solution pathway will lead to a dead end	Changing from one solution pathway to a different solution pathway

*Heuristic Strategies

Appropriate strategy initially selected	Data organized	Multiple Strategies used to make progress or clarify	No heuristic used

Verification

Checked if answer was reasonable	checked correctness of answer	Checked for errors in solution	No verification used

Mathematical Practices and Habits: Solution (is)

Based on reason/logic	Thorough/Complete	Neatly organized	Attended to Precision	Correct

Resources: Knowledge is

Complete	Sound with minor errors	Some but significant faults appear	No knowledge

Beliefs and Attitudes: Problem Solver Exhibited

Persistence	Confidence	Curiosity

Geiger, V., & Galbraith, P. (1998). Developing a diagnostic framework for evaluating student approaches to applied mathematics. *International Journal of Mathematics, Education, Science, and Technology*, 29. 533-559.

Teachers must expect *rigorous solutions* from students rather than just writing a final answer on a blank line. Students will write coherent, complete, convincing arguments. Solutions vs. Answers: What does RIGOR look like?

- A **solution** to a problem should:

    o   Supply reasons or explanations or other notes to clarify the work presented.

    o   Demonstrate understanding of the methods involved.

    o   Communicate what has been done and why:

- Any written **solution**, when read by you, other classmates, the instructor, or grader, will lead the reader to say `I understand how that was done', based on what is written.

- Numerical, or yes/no **answers,** like the **answers** at the back of the book are <u>not</u> solutions.

Consider the functions $f(x) = x^2 - 4x$ and $g(x) = 2x + 16$.

Solve $f(x) = g(x)$ algebraically showing all steps.

This is considered a mathematical *solution:*

$$f(x) = g(x)$$
$$x^2 - 4x = 2x + 16$$
$$x^2 - 4x - 2x - 16 = 0$$
$$x^2 - 6x - 16 = 0$$
$$(x-8)(x+2) = 0$$
$$x - 8 = 0 \quad OR \quad x + 2 = 0$$

The answer: $x = 8 \quad OR \quad x = -2$

The solution justifies and contains the answer.

Note to the Reader: When my former students are asked what lessons or habits they use in their professional life a very frequent response is the ability to craft a convincing (mathematical) argument. Two definitions that will guide your day-to-day performance expectations are given by Goldin and DeBellis (1999):

Mathematical Integrity: An insistence that a solution is mathematically adequate and makes sense; and

Mathematical Intimacy: Willingness to take risks, persevere, and have confidence.

Introduce Template and Camera-Ready Expectations
Teacher-Generated Classroom Innovations

Two outcomes of my past summer workshop experiences were the teacher-generated products called the Camera-Ready Expectations (and posters) and the Problem-Solving Template (PST).

During workshop sessions, teachers were regularly called on by the facilitator to share their work at the document camera or white board. The following expectations for thework, called "Camera-Ready" by the facilitator were used as talking points for peer feedback.

The facilitator always began critiques with "What did you like about her/his presentation?" to give positive feedback to all presenters whether they answered the problem correctly or not. Samples of peer comments included "I liked that she showed every step in her thinking," or "I liked his use of precise units and labels." If improvements could be made the facilitator asked audience members," How can he/she put the plus on his/her A?" Vicich and Clark (2016) notedthat the phrase '**Camera-Ready'** became a "taken-as-shared mathematical practice established by the classroom community" as described by Cobb and Yackel (1998). AMP teachers use the phrase 'Camera-Ready' in their normal classroom discourse and some have posters they have created displayed in their classroom . "The poster is a combination of my AMP experiences and the 7c's of creativity used at [my school] by teachers and students. The 7c's are cogitate, collaborate, calculate, craft, construct, communicate, and connect. " Note: The word 'craft' for Julia meant the art of communicating.

Oral presentations made with the aid of a doc camera offered several opportunities for shared practices. These included use of precise language and vocabulary, use of proper notation,a verification component in a solution, reinforcement of common procedural skills and algorithms but also opportunities to present alternative solution pathways that may have been clever or elegant. Often times teachers remarked when seeing an alternative solution pathway, "I didn't think of solving the problem that way myself."

At the end of a summer week of professional development, two teachers created and shared their first versions of a ***Problem-Solving Template*** (PST) designed as a graphic organizer to provide structure to their own students. The categories of problem-solving behaviors of *identify given and goals, make plans and conjectures, justification, final answer as a complete sentence and verification* were organized into boxes on a two-sided handout. The facilitator intervened and suggested including a grading rubric for giving students feedback. The rubric would communicate the value of developing productive behaviors and habits of mind without necessarily getting the final answer correct. A second generation of PSTs that included grading rubrics emerged and was shared at subsequent workshops. A third generation included strategies, and guiding questions to help students make progress.

In a recent survey of AMP participants (n = 81), 95% of teachers reported using some form of the PST during the school year. 69% of those using a PST preferred to use it more frequently at the beginning of year to establish quality of work expectations and "to get them thinking like a problem solver."

Teachers used the PST throughout the year to "help students maintain productive habits as well as promote organizational skills and consistency in their work. Some teachers had blank templates available throughout the year and other teachers prefer that students "eventually create camera-ready work without it."

Vicich, J. (2018). Professional development for improving middle school teachers' and students' problem-solving skills: Guidelines and resources for coaches and teachers. Retrieved Jan. 9, 2024: http://www.mspnet.org/library/33498.html.

Created by Ashley Jimenez

GOAL:

GIVENS:

Name: _____________________

Period: _____ Date: __________

Conjecture:

Plan: What strategies will you use? Keywords

Solution (show all work, label):

Verification (at least 2 sentences):

Answer (written as a complete sentence with units!!):

Goal/Givens	Conjecture	Plan/Strategies	Solution	Verification	Correct Answer	Com. Sen.
1 pt	1 pt	1 pts	2 pts	2 pts	2 pts	1 pt

Created by Keith Rogers and Dr. James Vicich
Problem-Solving Template
Problem Statement here: Name ____

Given(s)	Goal(s)

Planning/Identify Sub-goals– Break the problem down into simple tasks

TOOLBOX: Formulas:

Strategy Selection:
1)   Draw and label a diagram if possible.
2)   Examine special cases:
   a. Select specific values to get a "feel" for the problem.
   b. Look for patterns.
   c. Examine limiting cases to explore the range of possibilities.
3)   Try to simplify the problem and/or exploit symmetry.
4)   Consider equivalent problems:
   a. Re-combine elements of the problem in different ways.
   b. Introduce auxiliary elements.
   c. Consider argument by contradiction
5)   Consider slightly modified goals and subgoals:
   a. Choose some subgoals to work on (partially solve the problem).
   b. Relax a condition and try to re-impose it.
   c. Exploit both *result* and *method* of similar problems
6)   Act out the problem or use manipulatives.
7)   Identify what does not work to eliminate possible solutions.
8)   Work backwards (from last line in solution to first line).
(Adapted from Alan Schoenfeld (1998)

Conjecture about the answer (Reasonable guess):

Answer (Written as a complete sentence with proper units and notation.)

Verification: Explain why your answer is reasonable and makes sense. Use mathematical reasoning to prove that your answer is correct.

Original Problem: <u>Underline the givens</u> and circle the goals.

Name

1

Date   Hour

Conjecture (reasonable guess):

Plan: What will you do to solve this problem?
(I am going to … so that I can …)

Questions for getting unstuck:

Have I tried the strategies and followed my plan?

Am I getting closer to solution?

Can I break this problem into smaller pieces?

Other questions I asked myself:

Strategy Selection:

1. Draw and label a diagram.

2. Examine special cases.

3. Simplify the problem.

4. Consider equivalent problems.

5. Consider slightly modified goals and   subgoals.

6. Act out the problem/ use manipulatives.

Solution Pathway (Not just what you did, but WHY you did it. Remember, your work is for everyone!)

Answer (Stated in a complete sentence, referring to the question, units included as necessary):

Check (verification): Use mathematical reasoning to prove that your answer is correct.

I know my answer is right because...

Underline the givens and circle the goals (1)	Conjecture and plan are appropriate and make sense in context of the problem (3)	Solution pathway is complete, questions are present; solution is checked for reasonableness and verified (4)	Answer is correct, and is stated in a way that responds directly to the question asked (2)	Total (10)

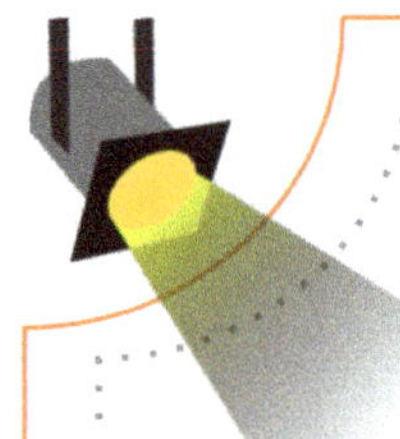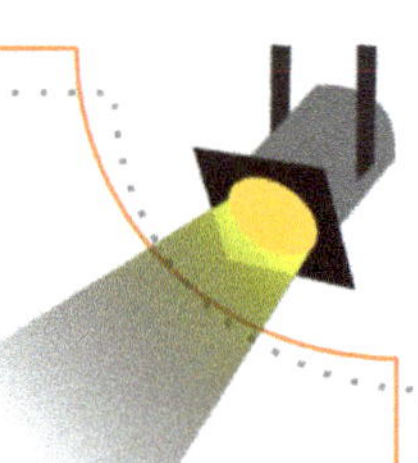

Is my work Camera Ready?

Perseverance, solution pathway(s)… ACTION!

Have I <u>underlined</u> the givens, circled the goals, and made a reasonable conjecture?

Do I have a labeled picture, model, or diagram?

Are my calculations and work precise with:

* units labeled?

* vocabulary that relates to the problem?

* an answer written in a complete sentence?

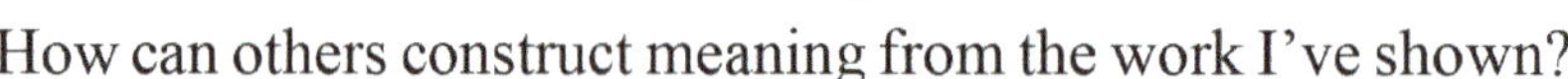

How can others construct meaning from the work I've shown?

How might I work connect to other ideas?

How my work could be used as a collaboration tool to improve my craft?

Part II
Problems for Various Strategies and Essential Content

If you are going to achieve excellence in big things, you develop the habit in little matters. Excellence is not an exception, it is a prevailing attitude. —Colin Powell

Excellence, then, is not an act, but a habit. —Aristotle

Notes to the reader:

Become familiar with each of the Frequently Used Heuristics and Strategies. Each problem in this section corresponds to a strategy or related content topic. The *PURPOSE* for each problem is stated above the problem statement, however, students may select an alternate strategy and arrive at a correct answer. Selecting an appropriate strategy is an important skill but creating alternate solution pathways is an equally important skill. The classroom culture should include expectations that (a) students will be engaged in mathematical discourse with the teacher and with fellow students, (b) students will be explaining their mathematical thinking, (c) students will be justifying their reasoning mathematically, (d) students will critique the thinking of others, (e) **the mathematics itself will be the ultimate authority** to determine the validity of a claim and students will need to convince their own classmates through sound and logical reasoning, (f) students will be engaged in problem-solving, (g) students will be communicating (verbally and in writing) mathematical thinking coherently and precisely (language), (h) students will be sharing alternative solution pathways, and (i) students will embrace mistakes and remain persistent when problem solving.

Effective communication in both oral and written formats is an extremely important instructional and performance goal. Student presentations should occur daily. The BORDER PROBLEM is used by some teachers on the first day of class to establish a culture of respectfully sharing and critiquing ideas of others and is a rich opportunity to develop different ways of thinking about a various solution pathways.

Frequently Used Heuristics and Strategies
(Adapted from Alan Schoenfeld (1998) and Vicich (2010))

Purpose: Learn to use an appropriate strategy to solve problems.

1) Draw and label a diagram if possible.
2) Examine special cases:
    a) Select specific values to get a "feel" for the problem.
    b) Look for patterns.
    c) Examine limiting cases to explore the range of possibilities.
3) Try to simplify the problem and/or exploit symmetry.
4) Consider equivalent problems:
    a) Re-combine elements of the problem in different ways.
    b) Introduce auxiliary elements.
    c) Consider argument by contradiction.
5) Consider slightly modified goals and subgoals:
    a) Choose some subgoals to work on (partially solve the problem).
    b) Relax a condition and try to re-impose it.
    c) Exploit both *result* and *method* of similar problems.
6) Act out the problem or use manipulatives.
7) Identify what does not work to eliminate possible solutions. (That is, find the complement.)
8) Work backwards (from last line in solution to first line).
9) Draw an auxiliary line and decompose complicated figures into component parts.

Note: While verifying a solution for mathematical correctness, one may ask: Does the solution:
    a) Use all pertinent data?
    b) Conform to reasonable predictions and estimates?
    c) Make sense?

*When using a mathematical argument to convince others, **first convince yourself**, then a friend, then a critic that your solution is mathematically correct and makes sense. Adapted from Schoenfeld (1987)*

Guidelines for Oral Presentations

Purpose: Learn to communicate ideas in written and oral form using precise language and proper presentation skills.

To the teacher:
- Use daily;
- Assign problems and partners during the previous session;
- First, find something positive to acknowledge; or ask the class, -
  "What did you like/appreciate about this presentation?"
- Ask the class and the presenter for ways to improve.

To the student:
- Provide a neatly organized, thorough written solution;
- Be poised, look and sound confident;
- Use proper body position so that the audience can easily see both your written work and your face;
- Maintain eye contact with the audience;
- Use a voice that is clear and appropriately loud for the setting.

Number Sense: Common Squares and Cubes

Purpose: Lynne Steen said that mathematics is the science of patterns. The perfect squares and cubes show up in many places within mathematics and must be a part of every student's number sense.

Complete the chart.

N	N^2	N^3
1		
2		
3		
4		
5		
6		
7		
8		
9		
10		1000
11		1331
12		1728
13		2197
14		2744
15		3375
16		4096
17		4913
18		5832
19		6859
20		

Can you find a pattern in the perfect squares' column?

Explorations and Extensions

Purpose: This problem motivates a student to draw a visual representation to help make sense of the problem. Additionally, a familiar pattern will emerge from a student's number sense.

How many squares are there on a checkerboard? Recall that there are 8 squares on each side. Hint: There are more than 64 squares.

Plan for exploration:

Solution:

(Adapted from: Johnson & Herr (2001). *Problem Solving Strategies* (2nd edition). Emeryville, CA: Key Curriculum Press.)

Problems that Illustrate Various Strategies and Heuristics

Purpose: Learn to draw and label visual representations. The essential mathematics concept is symmetry.

1. Students from Mr. Johnson's 7th grade class are standing in a circle. Each student is given a whole number then stands in numerical order. Consecutive numbering begins with one. The student holding number 6 is directly opposite the student holding number 19. How many students are in Mr. Johnson's class? *(Make a labeled drawing.)*
   Follow-Up: Which student is standing directly across from the student assigned the number 15? Provide a convincing, coherent mathematical argument.

Purpose: Create a coherent argument when no known algorithm is not available.

2. SHIP PROBLEM: Circa 1875: Twelve ships will leave San Francisco, one per month, to travel around the horn of South America bound for New York. At the same time, twelve different ships will leave New York, one per month, along the same route bound for San Francisco. Excluding meetings in the harbors, how many times will ships headed in opposite directions pass each other on the open seas? Each ship will take six months to reach its destination.

   Make a visual representation of the given information.
   (Create a solution path when no known algorithm is available.)

Purpose: Create an organized chart/table and use patterns to verify the answer.

3. COIN PROBLEM: You have a large bottle of coins (quarters, dimes, nickels, and pennies). How many distinct ways can a person make a total of $0.30? For example, three dimes is one way, and one quarter and one nickel is another way. *(Make an organized chart and look for patterns.)*

Purpose: Create an organized chart with appropriate labels. The essential math concept is counting consecutive whole numbers in a sequence.

4. DIGIT PROBLEM: A textbook is numbered from page 1 through page 1100. How many digits were used in numbering the pages? Recall, 0, 1, 2, … 9 are digits. *(Make an organized chart.)*

Purpose: This problem requires that students make a conjecture about the nature of the answer (A large number? How large?) and to make a plan BEFORE writing a solution.

Use of Conjecture, Estimation, and Measurement

1. If each person on Earth (approximately 8 billion people) were given enough space to stand comfortably on the ground without touching anyone else, estimate the length of the side of a square that would contain everybody in this fashion. Hint*: We assign each person a square of three feet on a side, and then arrange all the people into a larger square.

    Can you make a conjecture about the form and meaning of the answer? Can you anticipate using a particular strategy to begin solving the problem? Can you anticipate any necessary calculations? Recall: One mile is equivalent to 5,280 feet.

* Teacher note: You may want to have students determine these "personal square" dimensions by actively measuring the necessary area for one person in your classroom.

Adapted from Adam, J. (2003). *Mathematics in nature*. Princeton University Press, Princeton, NJ.

Use of Counterexample

Determine if the following propositions are true or false. Given a, b, c, and d are Real Numbers.

1. $\dfrac{a}{b} + \dfrac{c}{d} = \dfrac{a+c}{b+d}$

1. $2^n - 1$ produces a prime number for all natural numbers $n > 1$.

2. $(a+b)^2 = a^2 + b^2$

Purpose: To refute the validity of a mathematical claim one only needs to find one counterexample.

Developing a Coherent Mathematical Argument
(Adapted from the Ma Study)

Imagine that your neighbor's child tells you that she has a new math theory. She explains that she has discovered that as the perimeter of a rectangle increases, the area also increases. She shows you this picture to prove what she is doing:

4 cm   4 cm   8 cm   4 cm

Perimeter = 16 cm   Perimeter = 24 cm
Area = 16 sq. cm   Area = 32 sq. cm

How would you respond?

Purpose: Establish the habit of answering each of the following reflective questions in the order provided.

Guided Problem-Solving Exercise with Reflection

A rectangular plot of land is to be fenced in using two kinds of fencing. Two opposite sides will use heavy-duty fencing selling for $3 per foot, while the remaining sides will use standard fencing selling for $2 per foot. What are the dimensions of the rectangular plot of greatest area that can be fenced in at a cost of $6000?

- Can you identify:
    - (a) the given information?   (b) the goal (what you want to find)?

- Can you make any conjectures about a solution path or the final answer? Can you make a plan?

- What formulas do you need to know?

- Monitor your progress. Are you moving ***closer*** to the solution?

- Do you need to break the original problem into smaller subproblems?

- Do you need to *graph? create a table? use your calculator? draw a picture? write equations?*

- Is your answer ***reasonable***?

- Can you ***verify*** that your answer is correct?

- Is your solution ***neatly*** organized so that others may easily follow your thinking?

Purpose: Most problems have more than one solution pathway to the answer. Practice the habit of making a conjecture about the most efficient solution pathway.

Alternative Solution Paths: The Extra Guest Problem

A host has prepared five rectangular ground beef steaks for dinner.
An unexpected guest arrives just after the meal has been cooked.
Find two different strategies for preparing the steaks so that each of the six people is given the same portion of steak.

Represent your first strategy using operations with fractions.

Represent your second strategy using operations with fractions.

Based on a conversation with Keono Gravemejer, 5/2004, Utrecht, Netherlands.

Purpose: Make a prediction using your mathematical intuition and then create a convincing argument to determine if your prediction was correct.

Developing a Coherent Mathematical Argument

Compare the length (L) of the arc of the large, upper semi-circle to the sum (S) of the shorter semi-circular arcs. Given: The diameters of the smaller semi-circles pass through center of the large circle and lie on the same line; and the end points of the smaller diameters are the center of the large circle and the endpoint of the large circle's diameter.

Is L > S?

Is L < S?

Is L = S?

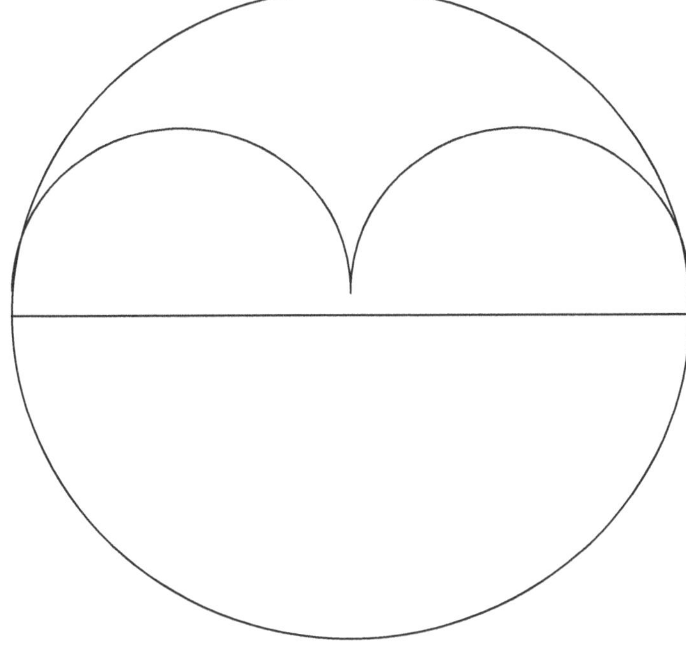

Try An Easier Version of the Problem/Bisbee Problem

A person makes a round trip from her home in Bisbee to her aunt's house in Yuma. Due to road construction delays her average speed on the way out was 30 mph, but her average speed on the way back home (with no road construction) was 60 mph. What was her average speed for the entire trip? Note: Mysteriously, the correct answer is **not** 45 mph. Provide an analytic solution to explain the mystery.

Hint: You may use a special case of "friendly" numbers to make progress on this problem.

Create Opportunities for Reflection: Playground Problem

Purpose: To increase a student's ability to reflect on her/his solution process, you may ask the following questions and listen critically to the responses:

What are you doing?

Why are you doing it?

How will that help you move closer to an answer?

Try this questioning technique on yourself while solving the following problem:

> Students at an elementary school had asked the principal to increase the area of their square playground. The principal doubled the length of each side of the playground. The children were disappointed that the playground area had only doubled. The principal told the children that if they thought more carefully about the matter they would be pleasantly surprised. What pleasant surprise would the children discover? (Adapted from the Ma Study.)

Focus on Mathematical Representation

Purpose: This is a typical problem found in a high school level algebra class and challenges students to label a drawing, make a plan, and monitor progress toward a solution. This problem can be solved by using the coordinate plane and selecting an appropriate point in the drawing as the origin.

What is the maximum area of a rectangle that can be inscribed in a right triangle of sides, 30 ft., 40 ft., and 50 ft. (see figure below)? The sides of the rectangle are parallel to the legs of the triangle. Think carefully about establishing a coordinate system with the origin placed at the most useful location. Write your answer as a complete sentence and provide a graph of the area function.

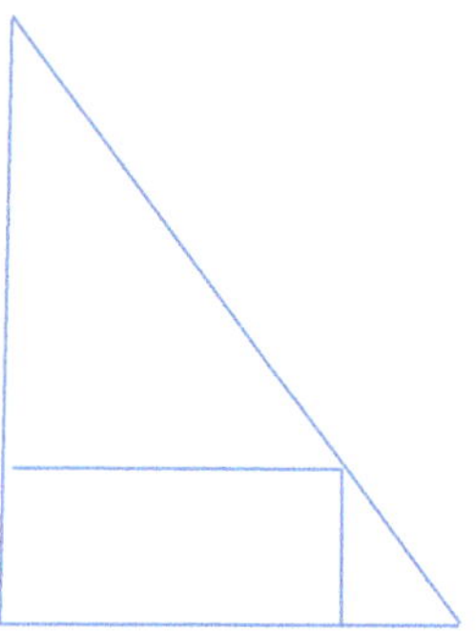

Resource Problems

1. A stack of 100 nickels is 6.25 in. high. To the nearest cent, how much would a stack of nickels 8 feet high be worth? (MT, 101(6)) *Purpose: Create a drawing to visual the given and goal.*

2. If you continued the triangular array of numbers shown below, what number would be directly below 122? Explain your thinking using precise mathematical language. (MT, 101(6)) *Purpose: Use your number sense to look for patterns.*

<pre>
                    1
               2   3   4
          5   6   7   8   9
     10   11   12   13   14   15   16
</pre>

3. How long will it take a two-mile long train traveling at 12 miles per hour to travel *completely* through a mile-long tunnel? Provide a labeled sketch to support your thinking. (MT, 101(6)) *Purpose: Create a physical model of this problem using a single sheet of paper.*

MT – *The Mathematics Teacher* is published by the NCTM, Reston, VA.

Benton's Problem: Focus on Subgoals

The two identical, adjacent squares have sides of one unit. Find the area of the oblique (that is slanted) rectangle. Show all steps. Hint: An excellent strategy is to label all vertices and redraw smaller sections of the larger figure for detailed subgoal analysis. (Adapted from the NCTM 100 Favorites Calendar)

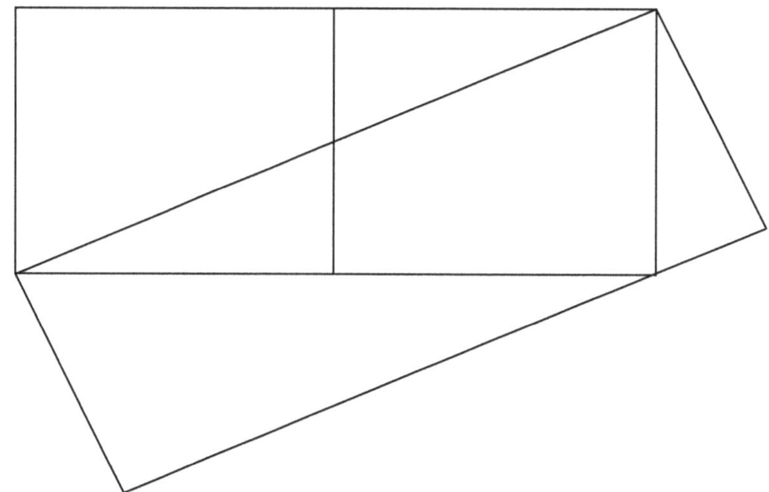

A Lesson in Notation and Deconstructing Complicated Figures

Purpose: Use a drawing to represent the given and goal. Use appropriate labeling to break the original problem into subproblems.

An athletic field with a perimeter of $\frac{1}{4}$ mile consists of a rectangular region with semicircular ends (Label the length of the longer side of the rectangular region L). Express the area of the field as a function of r, the radius of the semicircle.

Enculturation: What Does It Mean?

The task of creating and nurturing the ***"mathematics classroom culture"*** in which students will have the experience of doing mathematics has the following characteristics:

- Development of a mathematical point of view – using mathematics to symbolize, abstract, model, prove or disprove conjectures, perceiving connections across problems and results, and creating knowledge that is new to oneself or the community.
- Emphasis on process as well as results – explanations of how ideas are generated are highly valued even when they do not produce solutions.
- Leadership and Authority – the teacher leads the class towards assuming responsibility for standards of completeness, coherence, and the conviction of mathematical arguments. Here the mathematics itself is the ultimate authority.
- Communication – the classroom setting encourages written and oral communication where ideas, not the person, are critiqued.
- Reflective mathematical practice – Is your argument convincing? How could you arrive at the same answer using a different solution pathway? Can this result be generalized?

Criteria for problem selection:

- Problems should be accessible on the basis of prior knowledge.
- Problems should be solvable or at least approachable in more than one way.
- Problems should illustrate important mathematical ideas in terms of either the content or solution strategies.
- Problems should be constructible without tricks.
- Problems should serve as first steps toward mathematical explorations and springboards for further problem posing.

Source: Arcavi, K., Kessel, C., Meira, L. & Smith, J. (1998). Teaching mathematical problem solving: An analysis of an emergent classroom community. *CBMS Issues in Mathematics   Education, 7*, 1 – 65. Providence, RI: American Mathematical Society.

The Border Problem

Source: *https://themathletes.wordpress.com/2013/10/07/the-border-problem/*
Retrieved 4/27/23

Purpose: This is an excellent problem to illustrate that a problem can have several solution pathways that lead to the same final answer.

Without counting one by one, determine how many shaded squares are in this 10×10 grid.

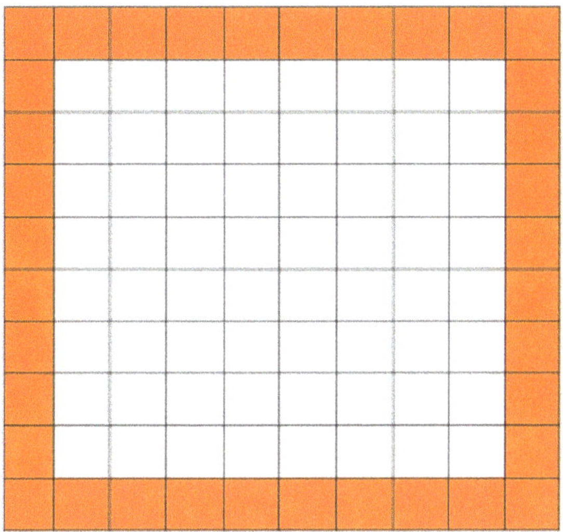

Record Students Methods and Ways of Thinking on the Board
Follow-Up Questions:
 What about a 6 in by 6 in grid?
 What about a 15 in by 15 in grid?
 What about a 253 in by 253 in grid?
 What about an *n* inch by *n* inch grid?
 Create a verbal representation
 Use the verbal representation to introduce the notion of variable
 If n represents the number of unit squares on one side, give an algebraic expression for the number of unit squares in the border.

Nice video YouTube video of the border problem and classroom discourse.
https://www.youtube.com/watch?v=Tgaah_0Urvs retrieved 4/27/23
Resource Problems: Nice Follow-Up to the Boarder Problem
Source: Mathematics Teaching in the Middle school • Vol. 19, No. 8, April 2014, p. 466.

Purpose: Examine a real-life situation and use previous experience (THE BORDER PROBLEM) to make progress.

The concrete for a sidewalk is being poured outside the perimeter of a new subdivision, which is a 280 ft. × 720 ft. rectangle. The building code requires that the sidewalk be 5 feet wide and 8 inches deep. How many cubic yards of concrete will need to be poured?

How much will the concrete for the new subdivision in problem 8 cost if the price per cubic yard of concrete is $120 and an extra 5% of concrete is being ordered?

Matt Weber Problem

Purpose: Use of auxiliary lines, decomposition, and subproblems to make progress. This problem relies on well-connected knowledge of the coordinate plane, geometry, and algebraic techniques for solving equations.

Given: A right triangle is drawn inside a 6-8-10 (inches) right triangle so that the margin between the two right triangle's parallel sides is one inch. Find the area of the inner (shaded) right triangle? Build a convincing mathematical argument. Note: The drawing below may not be proportional. Begin this problem with a shared labeling system of the vertices so that solution pathways can be compared with precision and accuracy.

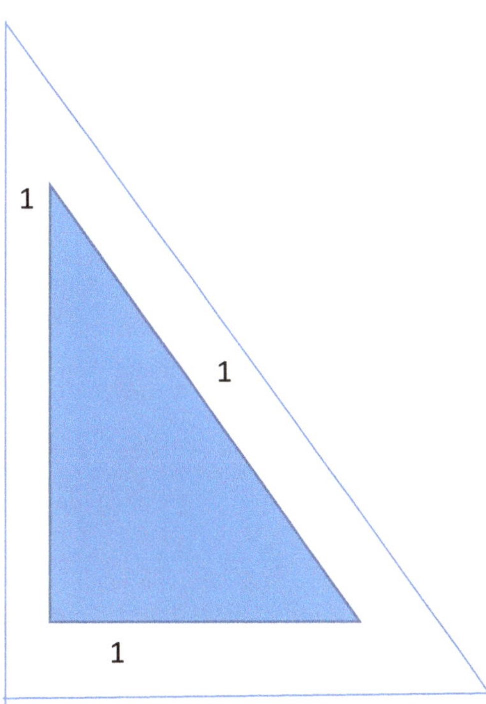

Purpose: These are guidelines for building productive mathematical practices by students and teachers.

Standards for Mathematical Practices (MP)

Arizona Department of Education Retrieved 5/17/21 https://www.azed.gov/standards-practices/k-12standards/mathematics-standards

1. Make sense of problems and persevere in solving them.
2. Reason abstractly and quantitatively.
3. Construct viable arguments and critique the reasoning of others.
4. Model with mathematics.
5. Use appropriate tools strategically.
6. Attend to precision.
7. Look for and make use of structure.
8. Look for and express regularity in repeated reasoning.

NCTM Mathematics Teaching Practices

Principles to actions: ensuring mathematical success for all. (2014). Reston, VA: NCTM, National Council of Teachers of Mathematics.

Establish mathematics goals to focus learning. Effective teaching of mathematics establishes clear goals for the mathematics that students are learning, situates goals within learning progressions, and uses the goals to guide instructional decisions.
Implement tasks that promote reasoning and problem solving. Effective teaching of mathematics engages students in solving and discussing tasks that promote mathematical reasoning and problem solving and allow multiple entry points and varied solution strategies.
Use and connect mathematical representations. Effective teaching of mathematics engages students in making connections among mathematical representations to deepen understanding of mathematics concepts and procedures and as tools for problem solving.
Facilitate meaningful mathematical discourse. Effective teaching of mathematics facilitates discourse among students to build shared understanding of mathematical ideas by analyzing and comparing student approaches and arguments.
Pose purposeful questions. Effective teaching of mathematics uses purposeful questions to assess and advance students' reasoning and sense making about important mathematical ideas and relationships.
Build procedural fluency from conceptual understanding. Effective teaching of mathematics builds fluency with procedures on a foundation of conceptual understanding so that students, over time, become skillful in using procedures flexibly as they solve contextual and mathematical problems.
Support productive struggle in learning mathematics. Effective teaching of mathematics consistently provides students, individually and collectively, with opportunities and supports to engage in productive struggle as they grapple with mathematical ideas and relationships.
Elicit and use evidence of student thinking. Effective teaching of mathematics uses evidence of student thinking to assess progress toward mathematical understanding and to adjust instruction continually in ways that support and extend learning.

Testimonial from a 42-year-old former student
now manager of a firm that installs giant wind generators.

Hey Dr V!

As for skills I learned in your classroom that I still apply today, I'd have to say the first one is sanity [of] checking my answers. I found with a lot of my employees, now that I'm in management, that once they get an answer to a problem, they take it as truth. However, something that you ingrained in my head was to make sure that it was the right order of magnitude or just plain made sense.

I would say second to that is I still use rate of change quite a bit. I had you for pre-Calc so we had an introduction to rate of change and I still use those types of applications all the time to see performance trends and how they change over time.

Finally, and probably most importantly, I think I can say that having to stand up at a whiteboard with a "juicy blue" marker and walk through the logic I used to solve a problem is a skill set that I carry with me today. When I did my Master's defense, or anytime I'm presenting a new methodology at work, I have people trying to drill holes in my steps. However, what I gained from your class was that if you go to present on a topic, you should know exactly what you're talking about and be prepared to defend your work.

Purpose: Excellent resource problems for using the concepts of Ratio and Proportion in the real world.

While sitting in his car at a train crossing, the driver decided to time how long it took for a 1-mile-long train to pass him entirely. If it took exactly 75 seconds for the train to pass, at how many miles per hour was the train traveling? What is your conjecture? Mathematics Teacher | Vol. 104, No. 1 • August 2010

The gas gauge on your car indicates that you have about ¼ tank of gas remaining. You buy $42 worth of gas at $3.949 per gallon, and now the gauge indicates that you have about 7/8 of a full tank of gas. What is a reasonable estimate of the size (or capacity in gallons) of the gas tank? Can you make a conjecture? MATHEMATICS TEACHER, Vol. 108, No. 4 • November 2014

THE BELT PROBLEM:
Integrating Algebra and Geometry

Purpose: This is an excellent problem for challenging a student's ability to make a reasonable conjecture and craft a coherent argument to verify or refute that conjecture. This problem can be solved with or without real numbers.

Imagine that there is a belt that fits exactly around the equator of the Earth. Now add one mile in length to this belt so that the belt is uniformly loose around the equator. What is the distance between the new belt and the surface of the Earth? Provide a convincing argument.

Guiding questions to ask yourself:
What mathematics do I need to access during the solution of this problem?
What facts[1] or resource knowledge do I need to solve this problem?
Can I relate this problem to a similar problem?
Can I make a reasonable conjecture based on my own experience or based on the solution of a similar problem?

[1] The circumference of the Earth at the equator is approximately 24,901.55 miles; and

One mile is equivalent to 5,280 feet.

Making Mathematical Meaning:
Unpacking the Quadratic Formula

Purpose: The quadratic formula is frequently used in mathematics but rarely do teachers give students an opportunity to unpack and make sense of the expressions contained in the formula.

Graph the function and then use the Quadratic formula to identify the roots.
Explain the meaning and interpret the graphical significance of all symbols used in your numerical results,

$$y = x^2 - 6x - 2$$

Requirements for Rigorous Graphs

Purpose: many real-life situations can be modeled by a mathematical function. A function can be represented by a table of inputs and outputs, a mathematical expression, or a graph. Be sure to label a rigorous graph with all vital components.

A graph must contain three elements per axis: Variable. Meaning and Unit

Draw a complete linear graph where *A* represents the altitude (in feet) of a plane at time *t* minutes since the start of the plane's descent, given, that the plane was ordered to descend from 32,000 ft. to 14,000 ft. at a constant rate over the next 15 minutes. First, provide a labeled table of inputs and out puts of at least four ordered pairs of coordinates including the first and last altitudes and establish the rate of change. Write a function to describe the plane's altitude since the plane was ordered to descend as a function of time.

Table Here:

Label axes, significant coordinates, variables, and units. Use a straightedge.

Meaning and Sense-Making

Purpose: Although this problem can be solved using calculus, one can explore relationships and make sense of the problem by creating a table of values and graphing those relationships.

Source: Hughes-Hallett, et al.6th edition. Calculus. Wiley & Sons, NY. P.338

A 747 jet needs to attain a speed of 200 mph to take-off. If it can accelerate from 0 to 200 mph in 30 seconds, how long must the runway be? Assume constant acceleration.

Note to Instructor: Be sure students include three types of labels per axis when using a graph: meaning/ title, variable, and units.)

Develop a Student's Curiosity

Purpose: Use a student's knowledge of the Pythagorean Theorem to make progress on this exploration.

Source: Mathematics Teaching in the Middle School, V21(1), August, 2015, p. 14.
NCTM, Reston, Va..

3. Is this assertion true: A semicircle constructed on the hypotenuse of a right triangle is equal in area to the sum of the areas of the two semicircles constructed on the legs? Explain how you know. (Hint: Don't forget Pythagoras.)

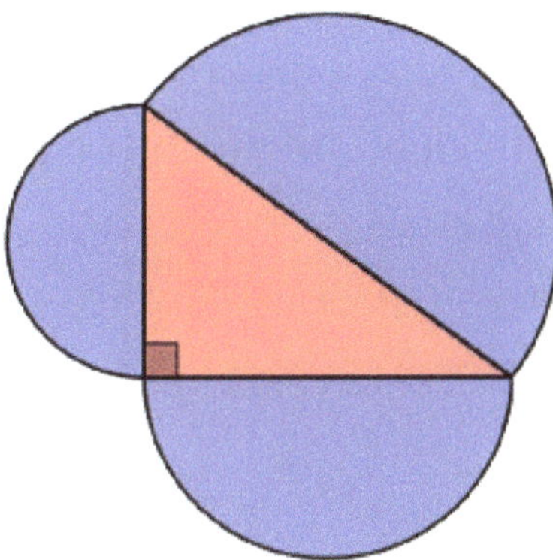

EXTENSION: Rather than construct semicircles, determine the validity of the proposition above using equilateral triangles constructed on each side of the right triangle. Provide a coherent mathematical argument to support your claim.

Lunch: The Pipe Problem

A large water tank was to be filled by one 8-inch diameter pipe. At the construction site, the pipe failed the inspection criteria and could not be used. A worker suggested that there were plenty of one-half inch diameter pipes available that would pass the inspection criteria. An engineer with a strong background in mathematics analyzed the replacement of the 8-inch diameter pipes by a *bundle* of one-half inch pipes and determined that the number of one-half inch pipes required was *unreasonable* and rejected the suggestion. What could have convinced the engineer to reject the worker's suggestion? Provide a mathematical argument with specific numerical evidence to support your claim. Note: There are approximately 231 cubic inches in one gallon.

Take-Aways and Look-Fors of Professional Growth Indicators for this Project:

The following five factors will be evident:

Factor 1—The classroom culture is very student-centered
Below are some specific characteristics of a student-centered classroom that would be evident to an outside observer.

- Students will be engaged in mathematical discourse with the teacher and with fellow students.

- Mathematical reasoning will be the ultimate authority to determine the validity of a claim and students will need to convince their own classmates through sound and logical reasoning.

- Students will be engaged in problem-solving and publicly share their mathematical thinking and respectfully critique the reasoning of others.

Factor 2—Teachers explicitly create learning experiences that promote the development of students' network/web of deep, well connected conceptual understandings. Procedural Fluency emerges from conceptual understanding.
This factor describes what teachers do to create a healthy student-centered environment. The questioning style of the teachers is a key factor. Teachers will ask questions of students rather than automatically providing the answer or explanation. Teachers will no longer be the final authority regarding the validity of a claim—the mathematics is the final authority. It will be evident that teachers are following an explicit process that involves the following:

Initial engagement and orientation to the problem that involves identifying the givens and the goals of the problem

- Pattern recognition and heuristics application

- Justification

- Generalization

- Defining multiple algorithms and solution pathways

Factor 3—The physical environment of the classroom will be conducive to student-centered teaching and learning
Key characteristics of the physical environment that will be evident include the following:
- Seating arrangement that facilitates communication among students

- Availability of technology and tools that promote the sharing of student thinking publicly (white boards, document cameras, etc.)

- Student access to manipulatives for exploring, communicating, and sense-making of mathematical ideas

Factor 4—It will be evident that students adhere to well-defined socio-mathematical norms
Socio-mathematical norms include the following:

- Each student is **expected** to share their thinking publicly.

- If collaborative work occurs, there is individual accountability.

- Errors are seen as opportunities for learning.

- Students feel safe to express their thinking—There is respectful communication among students.

- Teachers have high expectations for the quality/rigor of the thinking of their students.

Factor 5—There is a professional culture among teachers that models the socio-mathematical norms expected of students
It will be evident from the observations of interactions among teachers that the following occur:

- Teachers are **expected** to share their thinking with other teachers.

- Errors are seen as opportunities for learning.

- Teachers feel safe to express their thinking—There is respectful communication among teachers.

- Teachers have high expectations for the quality/rigor of their own thinking and the thinking of their colleagues.

*2014. Adapted from working documents of the Arizona Mathematics Partnership. A National Science Foundation Grant# 1103080.

Carlson's Paper Fold Problem

Purpose: This problem requires perseverance and a willingness to explore components of a complicated figure.

A square piece of paper ABCD, 4 in. by in., is white on one side and yellow on the other side. Corner A is folded over to a point A' that lies on the diagonal AC such that the total visible area of the paper is exactly one-half white and exactly one-half yellow. How far is A' from the fold line as measured along the diagonal AC?

Adapted from Carlson, M. (2000). A study of the mathematical behaviors of mathematicians: The role of metacognition and mathematical intimacy in solving problems. In T. Nakahara & M. Koyama (Eds.), *Proceedings of the Twenty-fourth Annual meeting of the International Group for the Psychology of Mathematics Education, Vol. 2*, (pp. 137 – 144). Hiroshima, Japan. (ERIC Document Reproduction Service No. ED452032).

Purpose: The problem below can be solved without calculus and may serve as a problem that introduces calculus concepts used in optimization.

Complete: Optimization Problem-Solving Process Organizer

- *Read the problem and identify the givens and the goal.*
- *Visualize the problem, and label the quantities relevant to problem;*
- *Find a formula for the quantity to be maximized or minimized;*
- *Use the conditions stated in the problem to eliminate variables; express the quantity to be optimized as a function of one variable.*
- *Find the domain of possible values for this variable from the physical restrictions in the problem;*
- *Use techniques of calculus and algebra to see if your results are reasonable.*

Example of Optimization Problem Solving:

A rancher has 3600 feet of fencing and wants to fence off a rectangular field that borders a straight river. He needs no fence along the river. What are the dimensions of the field that has the largest area? Provide a labeled graph of the area function to supplement your analytic (algebraic) solution. Use calculus to solve this problem. Can you make a *conjecture* about the answer?

Optimization Problem Solving Packet*

Purpose: Practice modeling various mathematical relationships and finding the minimum or maximum value.

Label quantities relevant to problem; 2) Find a formula for the quantity to be maximized or minimized; 3) Use the conditions stated in the problem to eliminate variables; express the quantity to be optimized as a function of one variable.

1. An open box is to be made from a 16 in by 30 in piece of cardboard by cutting out squares of equal size from the four corners and bending up the sides.
What size square would produce a box with maximum volume?

2. Find the dimensions of the rectangle of greatest area that can be inscribed in a semicircle of radius R.

3. Find a point on the curve, $y = x^2$, that is closest to the point (18, 0).

4. A cone shaped drinking cup is to hold 10 cubic cm of water. Find the height and radius of the cup that will require the least amount of paper.

5. A trough with a trapezoidal cross section is to be made to the given dimensions. Only the angle θ can be varied. What value of θ will give the trough its maximum volume?

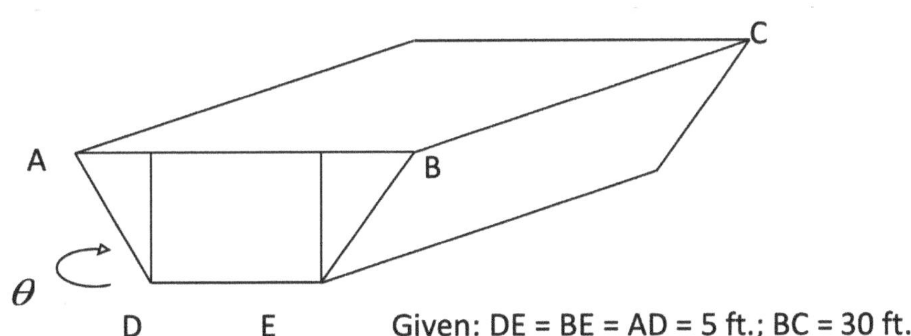

6. A wire of length 12 ft. can be bent into either a circle or square or may be cut into two pieces to make both. How much wire should be used for the circle if the area enclosed by the wire is to be maximized?

Initial conjecture:____

*Adapted from Hughes-Hallett, D., et al. (2013). Calculus (6th edition). NY: Wiley & Sons

Exercise: Diagnose Problem-Solving Behaviors

Purpose: Use the Diagnostic Instrument to analyze productive problem-solving behaviors.

Source: Mathematics Teacher, Vol. 108 (5), January 2015, p. 361. NCTM.   Reston, Va.

Two circles "fit" perfectly in a 2 x 1 rectangle because each
can be inscribed in a 1 x 1 square. What fraction of the rectangle's area lies within the two circles?

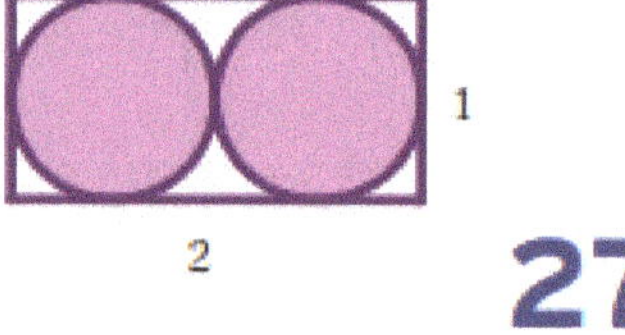

Note: To access the journals used in this packet, use: www.nctm.org,
and use the pull-down tab for Journals & Books. Log in, and then select either Mathematics Teaching
for Middle School, or Mathematics Teacher.

Bloom's Triangle Problem

Purpose: This problem requires perseverance and a willingness to explore components of a complicated figure.

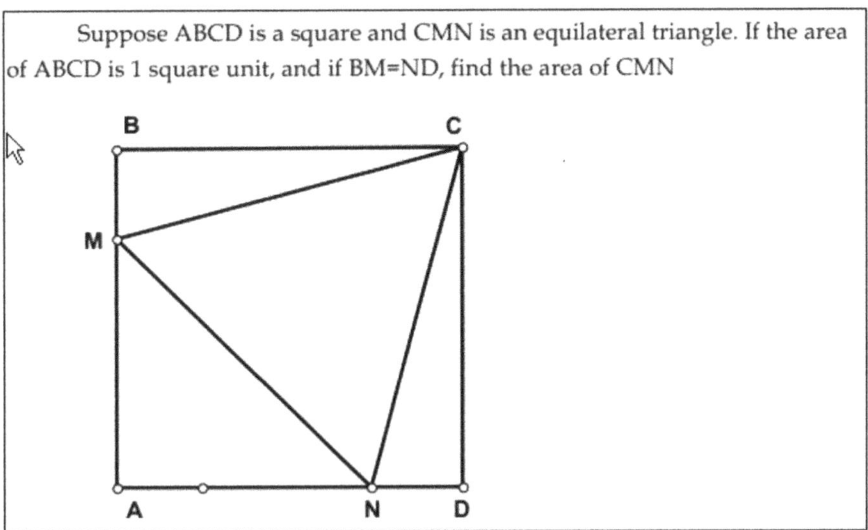

Bloom, I. (2008). *Promoting and characterizing the problem-solving behaviors of prospective high school mathematics teachers.* Unpublished doctoral dissertation, Arizona State University, Tempe, p.378.

Focus on Labeling a Graph (with meaning, units, and coordinates)
Adapted from Hughes-Hallett, Calculus. (Kalamazoo Problem)

Purpose: This atypical problem requires that a solver focus on the given and the goal.

You drive at a constant speed from Chicago to Detroit, a distance of 275 miles. About 120 miles from Chicago you pass through Kalamazoo, Michigan. Sketch a (labeled) graph of your distance from Kalamazoo as a function of time.

The Roof Problem
(adapted from released Smarter Balanced Items, NSF, DC., 2013)

Given: The schematic drawing of a roof structure. Segments AG = 6 feet, CE = 12 feet, GF = 2 feet, and   FE = 12 inches. Find the length of segment FB. Write any assumptions you make and provide a thorough mathematical justification that will convince the reader. Write your answer as a complete sentence. Note: The schematic may not be accurately drawn to scale.

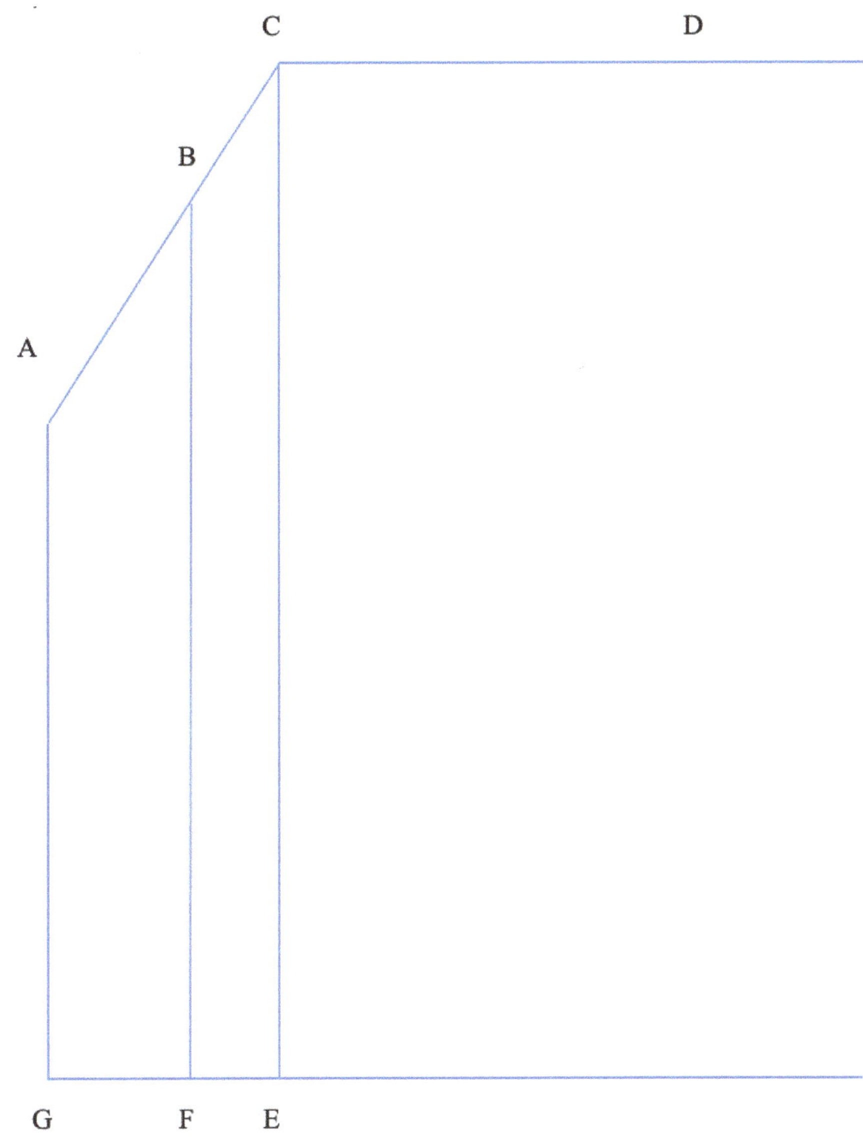

Assumptions: ____

Answer:____

Source: MATHEMATICS TEACHING IN THE MIDDLE SCHOOL, Vol. 19, No. 6, February 2014, p. 335, NCTM, Reston, Va.

16. The smaller of the two squares in the figure below has a perimeter of 8 centimeters. The larger of the two squares has an area of 25 square centimeters. What is the distance from point *A* to point *B*?

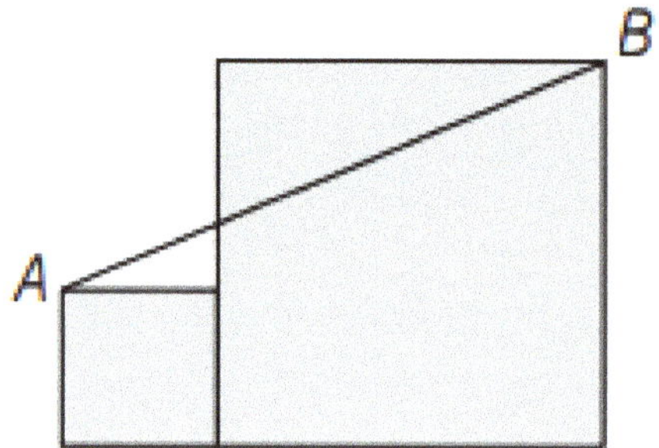

What does research tell us about students' problem-solving abilities?

Research on problem solving often compares students' performance to expert mathematicians' behaviors using theoretical frameworks grounded in empirical evidence.
Expert mathematicians have:

- access to rich, well-connected resource knowledge of facts and problem-solving experiences;
- an ability to imagine and make conjectures about possible solution paths;
- an ability to monitor their progress and dynamically revise or abandon solution paths;
- an ability and willingness to verify that a solution is reasonable and makes sense in the context of the problem statement; and
- confidence based on previous successful problem-solving experiences (Carlson & Bloom, 2005; Carlson, 2000; DeFranco, 1996).

In contrast to experts, advanced senior high students (Geiger & Galbraith, 1998)
and even graduate students (Carlson, 1999) exhibit weak ability to monitor their progress and reflect on results during problem solving. Unproductive beliefs that result from classroom experiences, such as "there is only one correct way to solve" any math problem (Schoenfeld, 1994) or rigor is not necessary since "the best solution always uses fewer steps" (Vicich, 2002) may impede students' problem-solving performance.

A recent, semester-long study (Vicich, 2002) of undergraduate developmental algebra students at a two-year college reported that these students' problem-solving behaviors were quite different from experts' behaviors. The developmental students infrequently planned a solution attempt, demonstrated an unwillingness or inability to consistently monitor their progress, and had varying degrees of success recognizing that a solution attempt was not making progress toward satisfying the goal of a problem. Furthermore, developmental students had varying degrees of difficulty switching to an alternative strategy when the strategy initially selected did not move the solver closer to a correct answer. With specific problem-solving instruction infused throughout the semester course, students earning an A, B, or C appeared to increase their willingness and ability to:

- identify the givens and goals of a problem;
- plan and verbalize their mathematical reasoning; and
- verify that their answer was reasonable and correct.

To help students develop problem solving skills overtly and persistently as part of each mathematics course instruction should provide students adequate time and frequent opportunities to experience problem solving in a variety of contexts, utilizing a broad range of resource knowledge, with prescribed time devoted to planning, monitoring of progress, and reflection on the adequacy of the solution and final answer. Students also need to solve the same problem using multiple approaches in order to build a resource of heuristic strategies but also to develop confidence investigating potential alternative solution paths. Problem-solving skills evolve over a fairly lengthy period of time (Lester, Garofalo, and Kroll, 1989), certainly longer than one semester for developmental algebra students (Vicich, 2002). Instructors should be aware that incoming college students have experienced significant challenges solving non-routine problems from elementary (Lester, et al. 1989) through junior high (Hart, 1984) and high school (Geiger and Galbraith, 1998; Silver and Kenney, 2000) and may need substantive instructional experiences to develop productive behaviors and mathematical habits.

Models for Learning and Teaching Mathematics

Unproductive	*Productive*
Teacher telling; students following	Initiative; Student investigations
Prevent mistakes	Make Mistakes and learn from them
Learn by listening	Learn by doing
Fear of mathematics	Curiosity and challenges
Teacher instructs	Teacher coaches
I "have" to	I "want" to
Look only at results	Look at causes
Others are responsible for my learning	I am responsible for my learning
Work alone	Work and communicate with others
Top-down design	Bottom-up design

Adapted from the work of Teo Kleintjes, R. O. C. Technical, Eindhoven, The Netherlands

Good questions to ask yourself during problem solving:

    What are you doing?
    Why are you doing it?
    How will it help you move closer to an answer?
    Does your answer make sense? Is it reasonable?

(Adapted from the published works of Alan Schoenfeld)

Problem: A Motivation for the Study of Algebra

Suppose you are offered a job in which you will be paid $1 the first day, $2 the second day, $3 third day, and so on. Naturally, you want to keep track of how much money you will have at the end of several days, weeks, or years. Visually organize a table and find a pattern of numbers to answer the following questions.

Day #	Day's Wages	Total Wages Expressed as a Sum	Total Wages
1	1	1	1
2	2	1 + 2	3
3	3	1 + 2 + 3	6
4			
5			
6			
7			
8			
9			
10			

1. Find the total amount of money you have earned after a) twenty days;
   b) one hundred days; c) two hundred fifty days (one year of workdays).

How To Solve It *(A Classic)*

Taken from the book, <u>How To Solve It (2nd edition)</u>, by George Polya, Princeton University Press, Princeton, New Jersey, 1973.

First: You have to understand the problem.
What is the unknown? What are the data? What is the condition?

Is it **possible** to satisfy the condition? Is the condition sufficient to determine the unknown? Or is it insufficient, redundant, or contradictory?

Draw a figure. Introduce suitable notation. Separate the various parts of the condition. Can you write them down?

Second: Devise a plan.
Find a connection between the data and the unknown.

Have you seen the problem, or a problem in a slightly different form, before? Do you know a related problem? Look at the unknown. Could you restate the problem? If you cannot solve the proposed problem, could you imagine a more accessible problem? A more general problem? A more specific problem? Did you use all the data? Could you think of other data appropriate to determine the unknown?

Third: Carry out your plan.
Check each step. Can you prove that each step is correct?

Fourth: Examine the solution obtained. That is, interpret the results.
Can you check the results? Can you derive the result differently?

Can you see it at a glance? Can you use the result or method for some other problem? Have you answered the question being asked? Have you assigned the appropriate units of measure?

Purpose: Finding Patterns

1. Make a table of pairs of numbers whose product is 60. Identify any patterns you see in your table. Is there a best way to organize your table? Explain.

   Provide two separate graphs each using appropriate scales.

2. Draw a rectangle whose perimeter is 30 feet. Label each side, and then calculate the area of that rectangle. How many rectangles are possible? Can you identify a pattern or relationship between the sides of the rectangles and the resulting area? What is your conjecture? Can you convince others that your conjecture is correct?

3. THE ROBOT PROBLEM: A man builds a robot, and programs the robot to build a clone of itself every five minutes. This new robot, in turn, can build a clone of itself every five minutes, and so on. How many robots are present at the end of thirty minutes? ... one hour?

   Hint: Record the results of your thinking in a table.

4. Given: (Hint: Can you create a table of ordered pairs, including some *x* values less than one, then graph those ordered pairs to see a relationship between *x* and *y*?)

TABLE

GRAPH

Independent, Open-Ended Mathematical Investigation
(Pizza Problem)

Your school district has asked you to write an independent research project for your students. You have determined that your students do not sufficiently see mathematics in their everyday lives. You supply students with the following information and ask them to make at least two distinct conjectures about the mathematical relationships that reside within the given information, then either verify or refute those conjectures. Your tasks as an instructor are to first motivate your students to be curious, and then be creative and persistent. *

Submit an instructor's answer key for this student project.

Given: The price of world-famous Romano's cheese pizza is:

12-inch diameter pizza costs $9.00
14-inch diameter pizza costs $11.25
16-inch diameter pizza costs $13.45
18-inch diameter pizza costs $15.45

* One of your students has come to your office after school to disclose that he has a fear of mathematics and needs some direction and encouragement for this project. You suggest that Romano's is considering offering a 9-inch diameter cheese pizza but has been unable to determine a fair price that is consistent with their other prices. You suggest that this investigation would be both creative and challenging. Include your solution to this special investigation. Be sure to provide a convincing, well-organized, thorough mathematical argument.

Handshake Problem:
Purpose: Pattern Awareness

Imagine you are in a room of people and that during introductions each person will shake hands one time with all of the other people in the room. How many handshakes will there be in the group?

Problem-Solving Strategy: Solve a simpler version of the problem; make an organized record of your thinking and results. Look for any patterns, then make a conjecture about the generalized form of the pattern.

Number of people in the room	Number of handshakes
2	
3	
4	
5	
6	
7	
N	

Describe a rule for determining the number of handshakes in a group of 4 students.

Describe a rule for determining the number of handshakes in a group of *n* students

Adapted from: Consortium for Foundation Mathematics (2004). *Mathematics In Action*, Boston, MA: Pearson

Strategy: Working Backward

The delivery of a very small package of medicine vital to the recovery of a terminally ill patient located in a remote town in Africa requires a 6-day journey from the nearest pharmacy. The medicine must be delivered by a person traveling on foot as the rough terrain will not support motorized ground travel (an air drop is not available). The weight of the medicine is negligible, and a person can carry the weight of only four days of supplies (including food and water) necessary for one person's survival. There are no sources of food or water along the journey. ***What is the minimum number of people*** required to get the medicine to the patient? Use complete sentences to describe your strategy for delivering the medicine. *(Hint: Work backward from one person delivering the medicine after a 6-day journey).*

A Farmer wants to build two adjacent rectangular pens for livestock. The pens share a common fence that separates the two pens. If the farmer has 822 feet of fencing find the exact dimensions that maximize the enclosed area. Provide an algebraic solution, a labeled graph of the area function, and use a complete sentence to communicate your findings. Use x to represent the length of the shorter side of the pens and y to represent the longer side of the pens.

Cottonwood Botanical Gardens plans to build a 6-foot-wide brick garden path around a circular flower garden of diameter 25 feet (see figure below, not to scale). The brick path is immediately adjacent to the outer perimeter of the flower garden. Calculate the area of the brick garden path. Show an exact answer first, and then provide an approximation to nearest hundredth. Provide a labeled drawing so that the reader of your solution can follow your thinking.

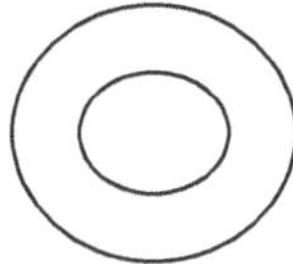

Reflections for Teachers
1. What mathematics do students need to solve this problem?
2. What difficulties will students encounter?
3. How will you know students understand the concepts?
4. How can this problem be *extended?*

The Loop Road Problem: A man drove one complete circuit on a loop road. His average speed was 12 miles-per-hour, and he took 15 minutes to complete the circuit. How many miles did he travel on the loop road?

A **small radio station in Telluride**, Colorado has a broadcast radius of 36 miles. How many square miles of listening audience does the station have? Population densities vary in that mountainous region. On average, the population density of Colorado is 40.5 persons per square mile. What conclusion can be drawn from this fact and your calculations?

Purpose: This is an excellent problem for discovering patterns and moving from specific cases to the general case.

SAMPLE NAEP Problem

Table 11.6
Extend Pattern of Tiles

Task	Percent Responding Grade 12

[General directions]
This question requires you to show your work and explain
your reasoning. You may use drawings, words, and numbers
in your explanation. Your answer should be clear enough so
that another person could read it and understand your thinking. It is important that you show <u>all</u> your work.

The first 3 figures in a pattern of tiles are shown below.
The pattern of tiles contains 50 figures.

Describe the 20th figure in this pattern, including the
total number of tiles it contains and how they are
arranged. Then explain the reasoning that you used to
determine this information. Write a description that could
be used to define any figure in the pattern.

Extended response	2
Satisfactory response	2
Partial response	18
Minimal response	29
Incorrect	25
Omitted	20

Note: Percents may not add to 100 because of rounding or off-task responses.

The following two pages include problems that offer opportunities to craft coherent convincing mathematical arguments taken from national assessment instruments.

Lubienski, S. T., Ganley, C. M., Makowski, M. B., Miller, E. K., & Timmer, J. D. (2021). "Bold Problem Solving": A New Construct for Understanding Gender Differences in Mathematics. Journal for Research in Mathematics Education, 52(1), 12-61.
Subjects: High achieving 8th grade students; and high school regular and college prep students

SAT Items on Problem-Solving Assessment (Studies 1 and 2)

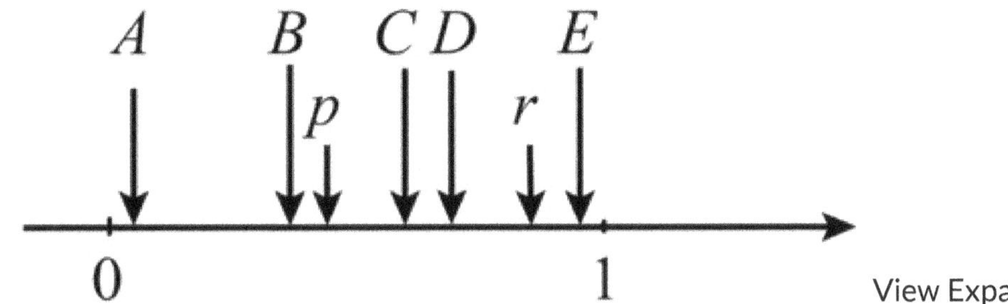

View Expanded

1. On the number line above, which of the lettered arrows could be pointing to the product p × r?

    o   a. A   b. B   c. C   d. D   e. E

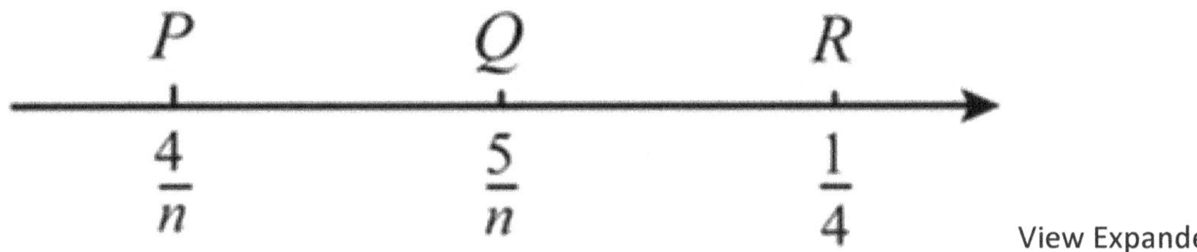

View Expanded

2. If the length of line segment PQ is equal to the length of line segment QR on the number line above, what is the length of PR?

    o   a. 112   b. 19   c. d. 16   e. 316

3. If x, 1x, y, 1y, z, and 1z are integers (positive and negative whole numbers, including 0), which of the following could NOT be a value of x + y + z x+y+z?

    o   a. 4   b. 3   c. 1   d. −1   e. −3

4. A blend of coffee is made by mixing Colombian coffee at $8 a pound with espresso coffee at $3 a pound. If the blend is worth $5 a pound, how many pounds of the Colombian coffee are needed to make 50 pounds of the blend?

    o   a. 20   b. 25   c. 30   d. 35   e. 40

5. The average (mean) of 5 integers is greater than 27. If the average of the first 4 integers is 22, what is the least possible value of the 5th integer?

    o   a. 32   b. 33   c. 47   d. 48   e. 49

(Note: These items were placed at the beginning of the assessment, followed by the five SAT items above.)

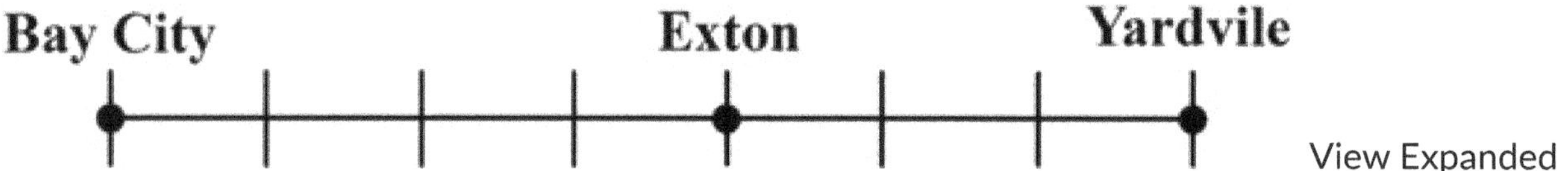

1. On the road shown above, the distance from Bay City to Exton is 60 miles. What is the distance from Bay City to Yardville?

   - A. 45 miles

   - B. 75 miles

   - C. 90 miles

   - D. 105 miles

2. In the past year and a half, Alfred's dog gained an average of 1/4 pound each month. Today, Alfred's dog weighs 75.5 pounds. How much did the dog weigh a year and a half ago?

   - A. 57.5 pounds

   - B. 71.0 pounds

   - C. 71.5 pounds

   - D. 74.0 pounds

   - E. 79.5 pounds

3. At the school carnival, Carmen sold 3 times as many hot dogs as Shawn. The two of them sold 152 hot dogs altogether. How many hot dogs did Carmen sell?

   - A. 21

   - B. 38

   - C. 51

   - D. 114

   - E. 148

Purpose: Explore connections between resource knowledge, curiosity, willingness to explore, and the skills of visualization and algebraic representation. The following problem was adapted from Hughes-Hallett, et al. (1994). Calculus (p. 295). New York: Wiley & Sons

A. The graphs of , , and bound a region in the first quadrant. Find the dimensions of the rectangle of maximum area that can be inscribed in this region. The sides of the rectangle must be parallel to the axes.

B. Find the dimensions of the rectangle of maximum perimeter that can be inscribed in the region described in part A.

Productive Problem-Solving Reflections:

- Can you underline given and circle the goal (what you want to find)?
- Can you make any **conjectures** about a solution path and/or the final answer? Can you make a **plan**?
- What **formulas** do you need to know?
- **Monitor** your progress. Are you moving *closer* to the solution?
- Do you need to break the original problem into smaller **subproblems**?
- Do you need to: Graph? Create a table? Use your calculator? Draw a picture? Write equations?
- Is your answer *reasonable*?
- Can you *verify* that your answer is correct?
- Is your solution *neatly* organized so that others may easily follow your thinking?

Part III
Learning Tools (Problem-Solving Templates, and Problem-Solving Performance Flowchart)

The quality of a person's life is in direct proportion to their commitment to excellence, regardless of their chosen field of endeavor. – Vince Lombardi

Note to the reader:

I recommend using any of the templates on the earliest days of a semester in order to help make productive behaviors habits of students that they turn to without prompting. I also encourage teachers to require that final answers be written as complete sentences that include proper spelling, grammar, and appropriate units.   Why?   The answer is that professional organizations require excellent communication skills from their members. Additionally, by writing a complete sentence the problem solver begins to reflect on the nature and correctness of her/his answer. Does that answer make sense to me?

The flowchart is a tool that is also especially effective at the beginning of a semester to encourage the problem solver's metacognitive reflection (thinking about the quality of one's own thinking).

Here is a version of the PROBLEM-SOLVING TEMPLATE that helps a student organize her/his productive problem-solving behaviors. The two examples of student work show how a template may be used. I recommend that you try and solve the problem first, then analyze how well the students performed.

The following samples of student work and problem-solving templates were developed by classroom teacher Jamie Stack who had participated in the Arizona Mathematics Partnership (AMP) teacher professional development program.

There are 270 students at Colfax Middle School, where the ratio of boys to girls is 5 : 4. There are 180 students are Winthrop Middle School, where the ratio of boys to girls is 4 : 5. The two schools hold a dance and all students from both schools attend. What fractions of the students at the dance are girls?

Goal: What fraction of the students at the Dance are girls?

Givens: The ratio at Colfax is 5.4, with 270 students. The ratio at Winthrop middle School is 4 5, with 180 students.

Plan: what strategies will you use? May have multiple checked. Circle the one that was most effective. (Plan is present & implemented in the solution.)

- [x] Draw and Label Diagram/Picture
- [ ] Look for patterns
- [ ] Write an equation
- [ ] Look for special cases
- [ ] Compare to a simpler problem
- [ ] Create model
- [ ] Make a chart
- [ ] Work backwards
- [ ] Other ______________

Conjecture: (reasonable guess)
$\frac{45}{100}$ of the students at the dance are girls

Solution: (show all steps throughout, label everything)

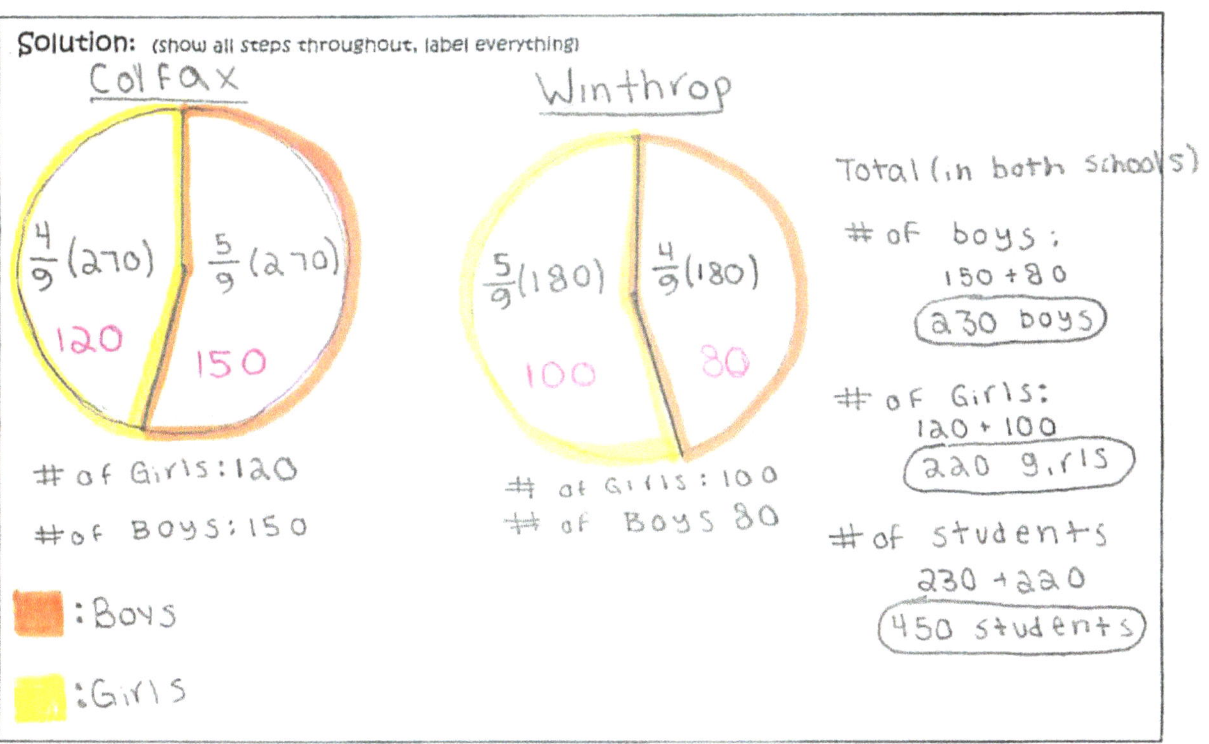

$4:5 = \frac{4}{9}$

Fraction (boys)

$$\frac{\#\ of\ boys\ (total)}{\#\ of\ students\ (total)} = \frac{230\ boys}{450\ students} = \frac{23}{45}$$

Fraction (girls)

$$\frac{\#\ of\ girls\ (total)}{\#\ of\ students\ (total)} = \frac{220\ girls}{450\ students} = \frac{22}{45}$$

Answer: (Complete sentence answering the goal. Include proper units, notation, etc.)

$\frac{22}{45}$ of the students at the dance are girls.

Verification: (Explain why your answer makes sense, why it is reasonable, is there another strategy/something different that proves your answer is correct?)

My answer is reasonable, because $\frac{22}{45}$ is a little less than one half, and if a fraction < 1 is taken from a large number, and added to a fraction > 1 of a smaller number, the result should be less than the remainder.

$$\left(\frac{4}{9}(x) + \frac{5}{9}(>x)\right) < \left(\frac{4}{9}(>x) + \frac{5}{9}(x)\right)$$

where x is greater than less than x.

There are 270 students at Colfax Middle School, where the ratio of boys to girls is 5 : 4. There are 180 students are Winthrop Middle School, where the ratio of boys to girls is 4 : 5. The two schools hold a dance and all students from both schools attend. What fractions of the students at the dance are girls?

Goal: What is the fraction of girls to all students

Givens: 270 students @ Colfax
The ratio @ colfax is 5:4 boy:girl
180 students @ Winthrop
boy:girl ratio is 4:5

Plan: what strategies will you use? May have multiple checked. Circle the one that was most effective. (Plan is present & implemented in the solution.)

- [ ] Draw and Label Diagram/Picture
- [ ] Look for patterns
- [x] Write an equation
- [ ] Look for special cases
- [ ] Compare to a simpler problem
- [ ] Create model
- [ ] Make a chart
- [x] Work backwards
- [ ] Other _______________

Conjecture: (reasonable guess) The fraction is $\dfrac{200 \text{ girls}}{450 \text{ students}}$

Solution: (show all steps throughout, label everything)

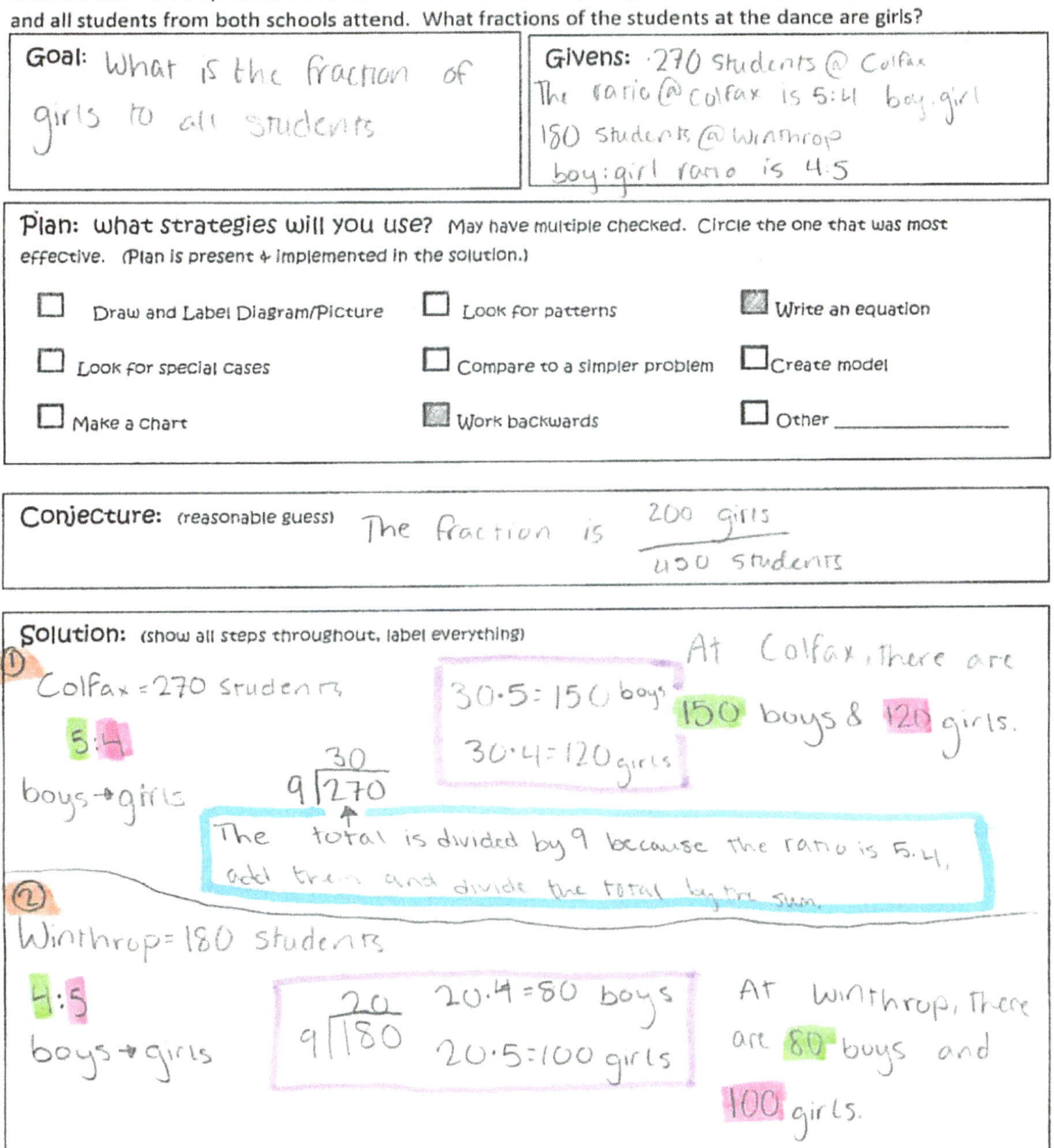

① Colfax = 270 students

5:4

boys → girls

$9\overline{)270} = 30$

$30 \cdot 5 = 150$ boys
$30 \cdot 4 = 120$ girls

At Colfax, there are 150 boys & 120 girls.

The total is divided by 9 because the ratio is 5:4, add them and divide the total by the sum.

② Winthrop = 180 students

4:5

boys → girls

$9\overline{)180} = 20$

$20 \cdot 4 = 80$ boys
$20 \cdot 5 = 100$ girls

At Winthrop, there are 80 boys and 100 girls.

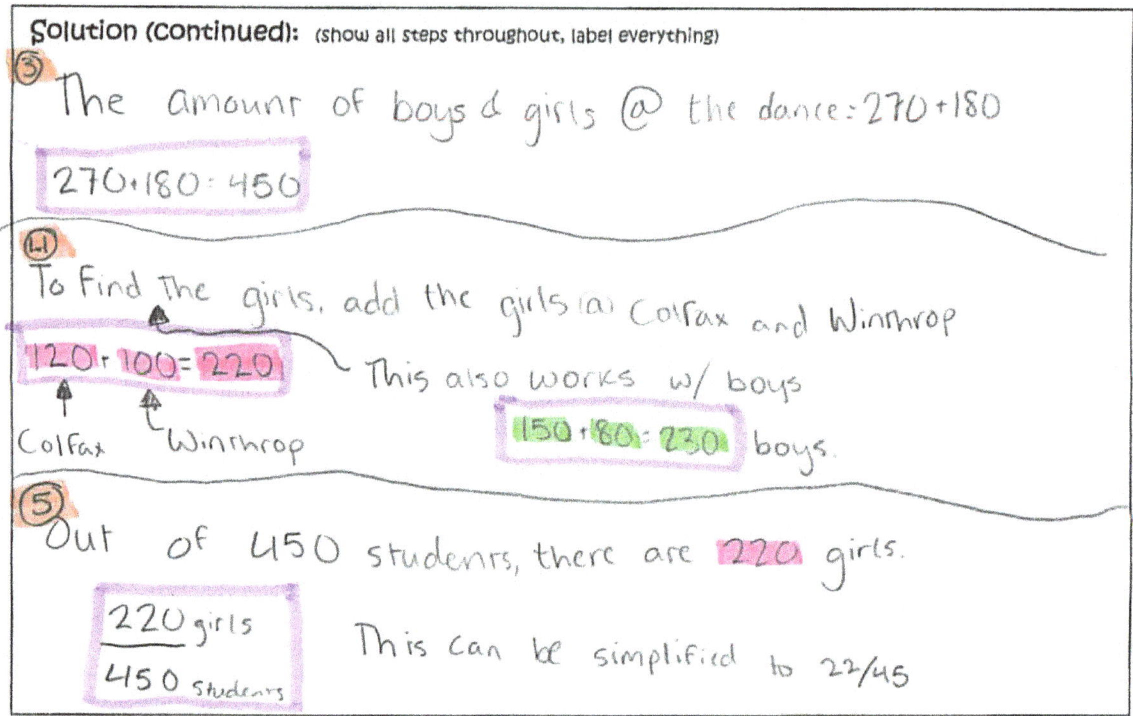

Answer: (Complete sentence answering the goal. Include proper units, notation, etc.)

The fraction of girls at the dance is 22/45.

Verification: (Explain why your answer makes sense, why it is reasonable, is there another strategy/something different that proves your answer is correct?)

• The fraction has to be girls/students because if it was g/b it would come out to ~95/100. That is incorrect as there are 450 students.
• If you disregard the # of students, and only use ratio, you get 9/18 for each. That is incorrect because for the fraction to be correct, the pop. has to be equal in each school.

Problem-Solving Performance Flowchart
We are what we repeatedly do. Excellence, then, is not an act, but a habit. - Aristotle

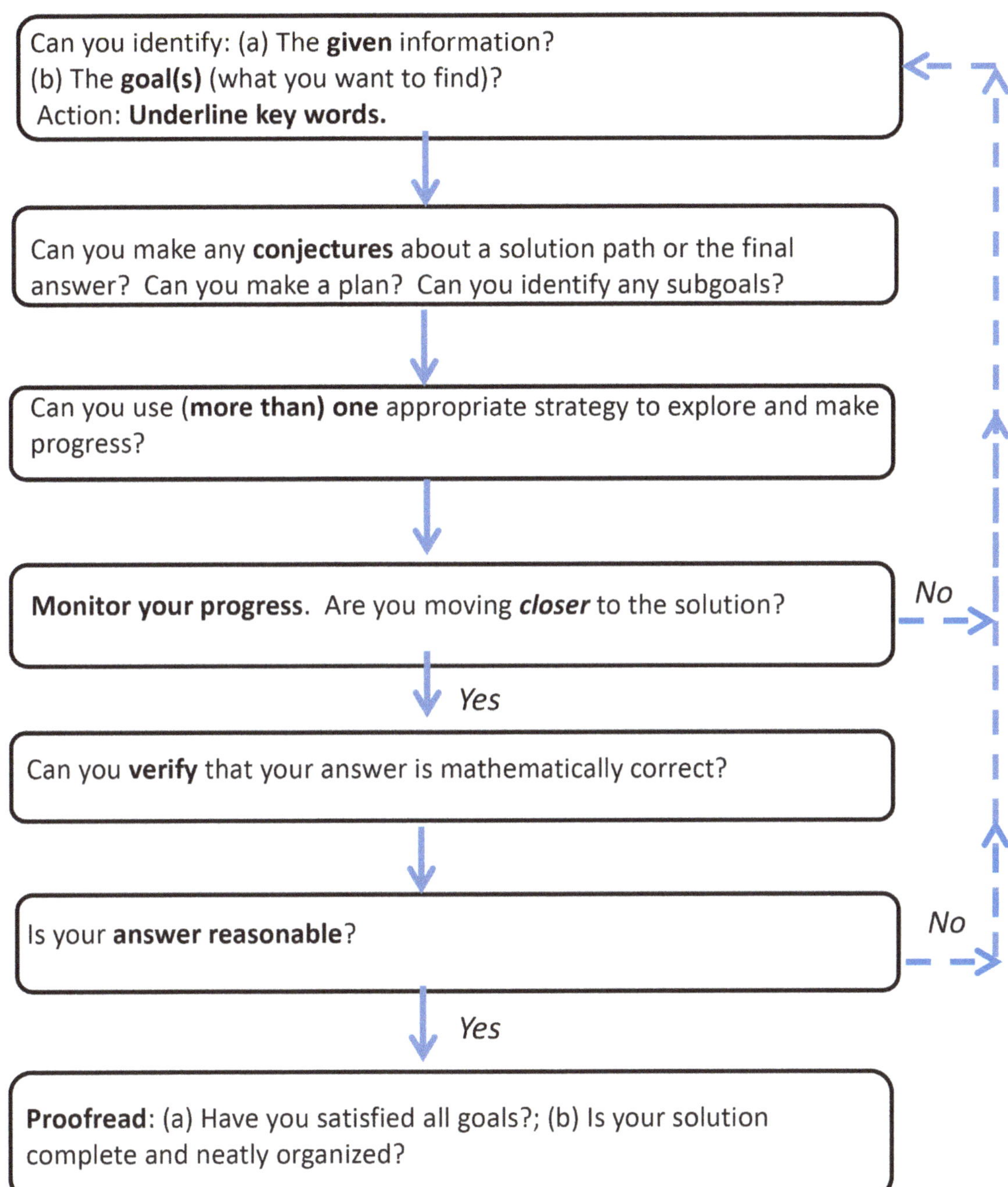

References

Carlson, M. (1999). The mathematical behavior of six successful mathematics graduate students: Influences leading to mathematics success. *Educational Studies in Mathematics, 40*, 237 – 258.

Carlson, M. (2000). A study of the mathematical behaviors of mathematicians: The role of metacognition and mathematical intimacy in solving problems. In T. Nakahara & M. Koyama Eds.), *Proceedings of the Twenty-fourth Annual Meeting of the International Group for the Psychology of Mathematics Education, Vol. 2*, (pp. 137 – 144). Hiroshima, Japan. (ERIC Document Reproduction Service No. ED452032)

Carlson, M. P. & Bloom I., (2005). The cyclic nature of problem solving: An emergent multidimensional problem-solving framework, Educational Studies in Mathematics, 58, 45-75.

Damon, W. (1984). Peer education: The untapped potential. *Journal of Applied Developmental Psychology, 5*, 331 – 343.

DeBellis, V.A., & Goldin, G. A. (1999). Aspects of mathematical affect: Mathematical intimacy, mathematical integrity. In O. Zaslavsky (Ed.), *Proceedings of the Twenty-third Annual Meeting of the International Group for the Psychology of Mathematics Education, Vol. 2*, (pp. 249-256). Haifa, Israel: Technion – Israel Institute of Technology. (ERIC Document Reproduction Service No. ED436403)

Geiger, V., & Galbraith, P. (1998). Developing a diagnostic framework for evaluating student approaches to applied mathematics. *International Journal of Mathematics, Education, Science, and Technology*, 29. 533-559.

Goldin, G. A. (1982). The measure of problem-solving outcomes. In F. K. Lester & J. Garofalo (Eds.), *Mathematical problem solving: Issues in research* (pp. 87 – 101). Philadelphia, PA: The Franklin Institute Press.

Hiebert, J., & Carpenter, T. P. (1992). Learning and teaching with understanding. In D. A. Grouws (Ed.), *Handbook of research on mathematics teaching and learning* (pp. 65-97). New York: McMillan.

Kazemi, E. (1998). Discourse that promotes conceptual understanding. *Teaching Children Mathematics, 410* – 414.

Kulm, G. (1982). The development of mathematics problem solving ability in early adolescence. *School Science and Mathematics, 82*(8), 666 – 672.

Johnson, D., & Johnson, R. (1992). Encouraging thinking through constructive controversy. In N. Davidson & T. Worsham (Eds.), *Enhancing thinking through cooperative learning* (pp.120 –137). New York: Teachers College Press.

Lester, F. (1977). *Mathematical problem-solving project technical report.* Bloomington, IN: IndianaUniversity. (ERIC Document Reproduction Service No. ED168834)

Liljedahl, P. (2021). *Building thinking classrooms in mathematics, grades K-12: 14 teaching practices for enhancing learning*. Corwin Press.

Ma, L. (1999). *Knowing and teaching elementary mathematics: Teachers' understanding of mathematics in China and the United States*. Mahwah, NJ: Lawrence Erlbaum Associates.

Rotella, R. (2008). Practice Like a Pro Golf 5 DVDs. Tour Practice, LLC.

Schoenfeld, A. (1985). *Mathematical problem solving.* New York: Academic Press.

Schoenfeld, A. (1994). Reflections on doing and teaching mathematics. In A. Schoenfeld (Ed.), *Mathematical thinking and problem solving*, (pp. 53 - 69). Hillsdale, NJ: Erlbaum.

Strom, A., Vicich, J., Cox, T., Watkins, L., & Romero, M. (2012). Promoting Excellence in Arizona Middle School Mathematics: Increasing Student Achievement through Systemic Instructional Change (NSF- MSP Grant #1103080). Washington, D.C.

Sfard, A. (1991). On the dual nature of mathematical conceptions: reflections on processes and objects as different sides of the same coin. *Educational Studies in Mathematics*, 22, 1-36

Vicich, J. (2002). *Mathematical problem-solving behaviors of undergraduate developmental algebra students.* Unpublished doctoral dissertation, Arizona State University, Tempe.

Vicich, J. (2007). Conceptual understanding, problem solving, communication, and assessment meet at the board. *Mathematics Teacher* v.100 (6), 420 – 425.

Vicich, J. (2014, September). Improving Problem-Solving Skills & Implementing the Mathematical Practices. Paper presented at the annual meeting of the Arizona Association of Teachers of Mathematics on Bringing the Mathematical Practices to Life. Tempe. Arizona.

Vicich, J. (2020). Professional development for improving middle school teachers' and students' problem-solving skills: Guidelines and resources for coaches and teachers. Retrieved 5/12/21: https://mspnet-static.s3.amazonaws.com/AMP_Professional_development.pdf

Vygotsky, L. S. (1978). *Mind in society* (M. Cole, V. John-Steiner, S. Scribner, & E. Souberman, Eds.) Cambridge, MA: Harvard University Press.

Selected Solutions

Checkerboard Problem

There is one large square (made up of 8 small squares on a side)   1
There are four squares (made up of 7 small squares on a side)   4
(Hint: Begin drawing a square, 7 small squares on a side from each of the four corners)

There are nine squares (made up of 6 small squares on a side)   9

Do you see a pattern of perfect squares? Continue the pattern.   16
                                                                          25
                                                                          36
                                                                          49
Finally, there are sixty-four small squares of length one per side.   64

So, there are a total of 204 squares on a checkerboard.

Mr. Johnson's Class

Key idea here is that only a *diameter* of a circle passes through the *center* guaranteeing that the endpoints of the diameter are truly *opposite* of one another. The strategy of drawing a representation of the students standing in a circle is followed by exploiting *symmetry*. There must be an equal number of students between the endpoints on either side of the diameter.

Fill in the numbers between the diameter's endpoints 6 and 19 and find that there are 12 students between the endpoints. Now counting backward from 6 to 1, complete counting upward from 19 until 12 students are located to achieve symmetry.

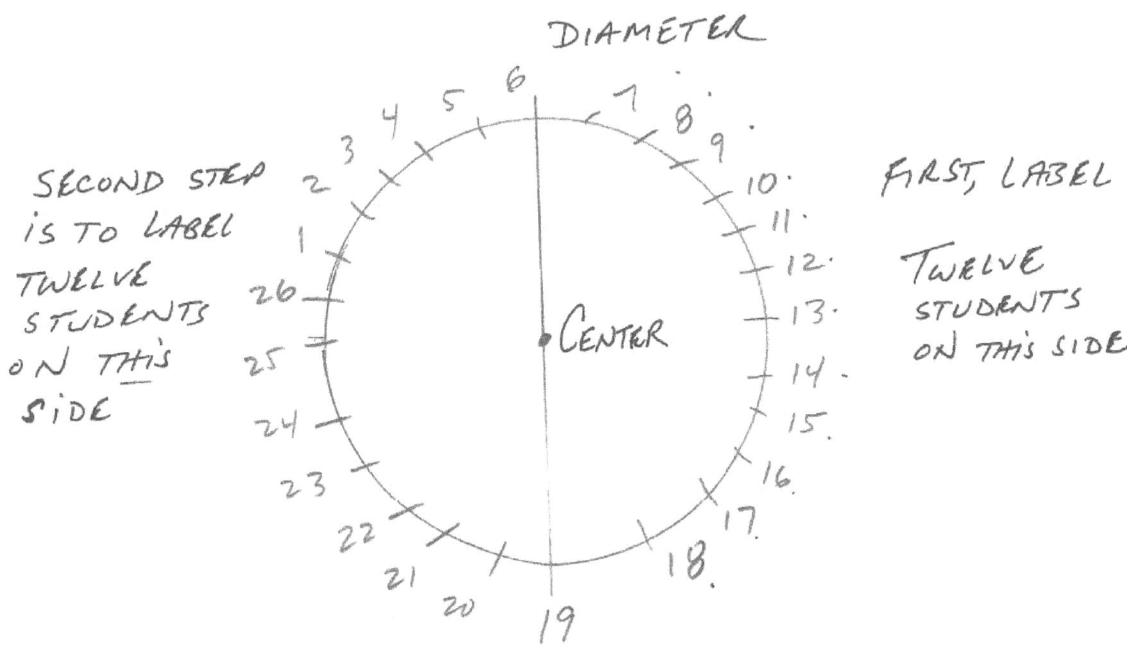

Coin Problem

A typical initial engagement, trying to make sense of the given and goal' is to record random combinations such as 1 quarter and 1 nickel, three dimes, and then 30 pennies. One quickly notices that there is no way to determine if all combinations have been found unless an organized chart is used to discover patterns. Be sure to notice descending and ascending patterns in the columns. Insert a zero rather than leave a cell blank so that one can determine if a sequence has been exhausted.

Q quarters	D dimes	N nickels	P pennies
1	0	1	0
1	0	0	5
0	3	0	0
0	2	2	0
0	2	1	5
0	2	0	10
0	1	4	0
0	1	3	5
0	1	2	10
0	1	1	15
0	1	0	20
0	0	6	0
0	0	5	5
0	0	4	10
0	0	3	15
0	0	2	20
0	0	1	25
0	0	0	30

There are 18 distinct ways to make thirty cents.

Note the descending pattern in the nickel column (6,5,4,3,2,1,0) and the corresponding ascending pattern in the penny column (0, 5, 10, 15, 20, 25, 30). Using the pattern one can see that all combinations have been found.

The Digit Problem

Focus on the importance of using an organized chart with appropriate column and headings and meaningful row labels. There are more than one solution pathways to the final answer, but each solution should be clearly labeled and easy to follow.

Key concept: Counting *consecutive* whole numbers in a sequence.
Strategy: Explore the problem with a simpler version, say, "How many whole numbers are in the sequence from 1 through 4?" The common incorrect attempt is to simply subtract, $4 - 1 = 3$. This attempt only counts the spaces between numbers in the sequence. To include the endpoints, one should use $(4-1)+1=4$. Verify: 1, 2, 3, and 4.
Try another sequence, say from 1 through 100. $(100-1)=99$ is incorrect.
Use $(100-1)+1 = 100$ is the correct answer. In general, when counting consecutive whole numbers in a sequence from *a to b*, the correct pathway is to use *(b-a) + 1*.

Use labels in an organized chart to help the reader easily follow your thinking"

	# of pages (b-a)+1	Times the # of digits per page	Total # of digits used in this sequence
Single digits pages 1 - 9			
Double digits pages 10 - 99			
Triple digits pages 100 - 999			
Quadruple digits pages 1000 - 1100			

Recall the goal: Find the TOTAL number of digits used in numbering pages 1 through 1100. By solving several subgoals (per row of the chart above), the solver is now ready to find the final answer.

Use of COUNTEREXAMPLE

Finding a counterexample to disprove a mathematical claim is a powerful strategy.

Can you find a counterexample to the claim: $(a+b)^2 = a^2 + b^2$ for Real numbers *a and* ?

Key idea: $(a+b)^2 = a^2 + b^2$ is an incorrect understanding often held by students that try to memorize formulas rather than understand relationships. Encourage students to be curious and explore relationships on their own. For example, this claim is disproved by choosing *friendly* numbers: let *a = 2, and b = 3*

 Then it follows that

$$(a+b)^2 = a^2 + b^2$$

$$(2+3)^2 = 2^2 + 3^2$$

$$(5)^2 = 4 + 9$$

$25 = 13$ but this false, so the claim is NOT true for all Real numbers. It only takes one counterexample to disprove a claim.

The Ma Study problem. Encourage your student to explore the claim by looking for a counterexample. Encourage students to be persistent as they may want to give up after only a few examples. Be creative, perhaps use numbers less than 1 such as 1/2 for the side of a rectangle.

Guided Problem-Solving Exercise with Reflection
(two-page solution)

goal: maximize area
given a fixed cost

$\$3/ft$ heavy

$\$2/ft$ std

Perimeter $= 2x + 2y$

Area $= xy$

$COST = \$2(2x) + \$3(2y)$

$\$6000 = \$4x + \$6y$

$6000 = 4x + 6y$

$6000 - 4x = 6y$

$\dfrac{6000}{6} - \dfrac{4x}{6} = \dfrac{6y}{6}$

$$\boxed{1000 - \tfrac{2}{3}x = y}$$

key idea: Focus on the Cost function

Recall   Area $= xy$

$A = x\left(1000 - \tfrac{2}{3}x\right)$

$A = 1000x - \tfrac{2}{3}x^2$

Rewrite $A = -\tfrac{2}{3}x^2 + 1000x$

To predict the graph of the area function,
a parabola that opens downward
with maximum area value
located at the vertex $x = \dfrac{-b}{2a}$

using $ax^2 + bx + c = 0$

let $a = -\tfrac{2}{3}$ and $b = 1000$

then $x = \dfrac{-b}{2a}$

$= \dfrac{-(1000)}{2\left(-\frac{2}{3}\right)}$

$X = 750$ <u>axis of symmetry</u>

Interpret these results and to find y
sub into the cost function

$6000 = 4x + 6y$

$6000 = 4(750) + 6y$

$6000 = 3000 + 6y$

$3000 = 6y$

$\dfrac{3000}{6} = \dfrac{6y}{6}$

$\boxed{500 = y}$

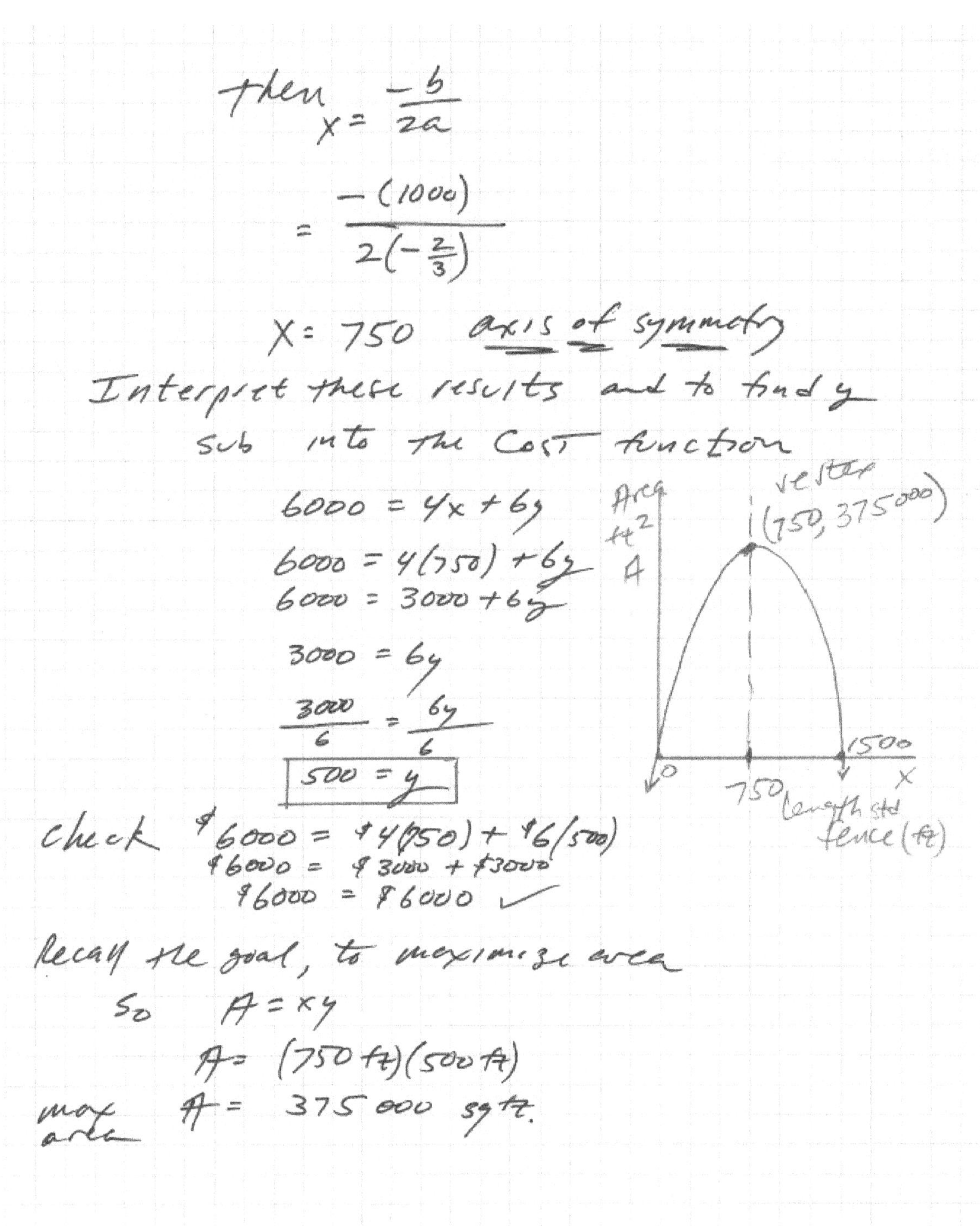

check \$6000 = \$4(750) + \$6(500)

\$6000 = \$3000 + \$3000

\$6000 = \$6000 ✓

Recall the goal, to maximize area

So $A = xy$

$A = (750\,ft)(500\,ft)$

max area $A = 375\,000$ sq ft.

Final answer: The maximum area of 375,000 square feet occurs when 500 feet of heavy-duty and 750 feet of standard fencing are used given the cost is fixed at \$6,000.

Alternative Solution Paths: The Extra Guest Problem

In a conversation with the highly respected Dutch Mathematics Educator, Keono Gravemejer, he described a real-life scenario in which he watched his wife solve a math problem at dinner time. The task was to make an equally sized extra portion from five ground steaks to an unexpected sixth guest's steak. ***Creating alternate solution pathways gives students the opportunity to strengthen a very productive problem-solving skill. Alternate pathways may appeal to readers/listeners of various abilities and also allows the problem solver to verify her/his answer in more than one way.***

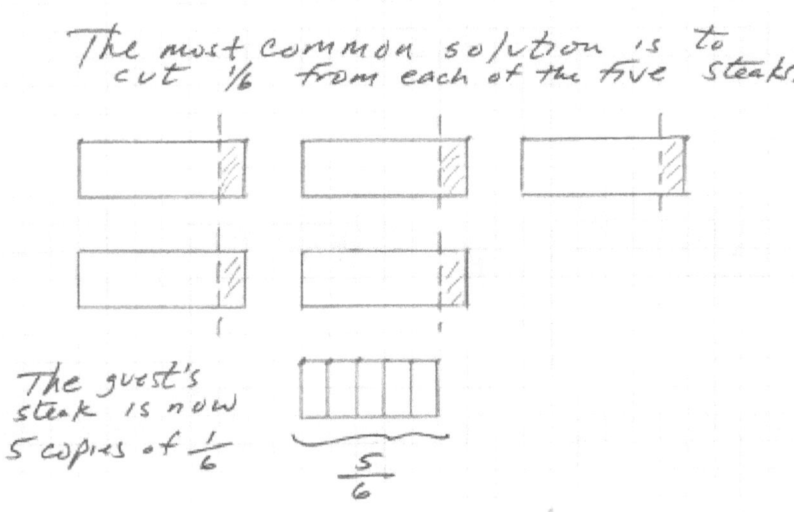

Mrs. Gravemejer chose to cut the original steaks into larger pieces for aesthetic reasons.

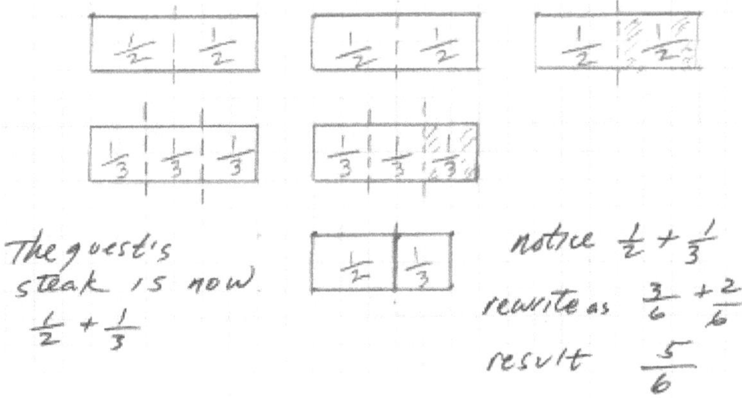

Bisbee

A useful strategy is to use *friendly* numbers to explore relationships within the context of a problem.

Imagine the distance one-way is 120 miles. The number 120 is friendly because it is divisible by both 30 and 60. So it follows that on the way out, using 120 miles, the time for the trip can be calculated by recalling:

$$\frac{dis}{rate} = time \quad \text{then} \quad \frac{120mi}{30mph} = 4hrs \text{ ; on the way home } \frac{120mi}{60mph} = 2hrs$$

So, the total time for the round trip is (4 hrs + 2 hrs) 6 hours.

Recall, $\frac{dis}{time} = rate$, using the total dis (120 miles + 120 miles) of 240 miles, and the total time (2 hrs + 4 hrs) of 6 hours, the average speed for the round trip can be calculated using:

$$\frac{240mi}{6hrs} = 40mph$$

Final answer: The average speed for the entire trip was NOT 25 mph but rather 40 mph.

Note: The common error when computing average rates is to use a formula without thinking about the meaning and relationships between numbers within the problem context. Erroneous thinking:

$\frac{60+30}{2} = 45$. Notice this is a procedural approach **without** attention paid to meaning or units of measure.

The Belt Problem

After identifying the givens and goal, ask the solver to write her/his conjecture about the answer. Conjectures can vary greatly from 1 inch to 100 feet to 100 miles. Two solution pathways are given below The first pathway uses numbers to calculate the goal. The second pathway uses variables to arrive at an exact answer and this pathway may be considered as *elegant*. Choosing appropriate labels or notation is a critical first step.

The drawing is not in proportion but is drawn to easily label the relevant distances and quantities. Let r = radius of the Earth at the equator; and let R = radius of the circle made by the belt uniformly suspended above the surface of the Earth.

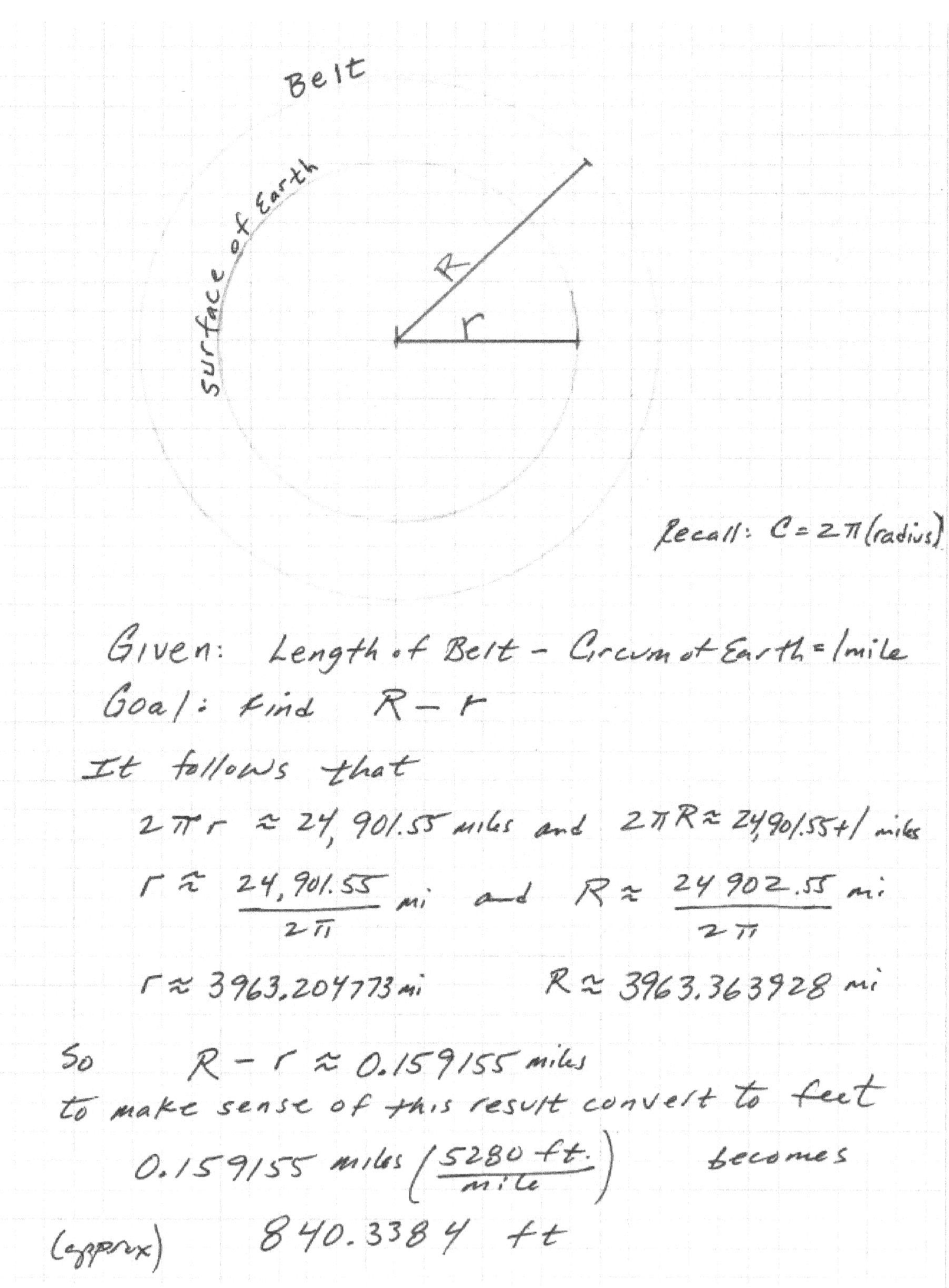

Given: Length of Belt − Circum of Earth = 1 mile

Goal: Find $R - r$

It follows that

$$2\pi r \approx 24{,}901.55 \text{ miles} \quad \text{and} \quad 2\pi R \approx 24{,}901.55 + 1 \text{ miles}$$

$$r \approx \frac{24{,}901.55}{2\pi} \text{ mi} \quad \text{and} \quad R \approx \frac{24{,}902.55}{2\pi} \text{ mi}$$

$$r \approx 3963.204773 \text{ mi} \qquad R \approx 3963.363928 \text{ mi}$$

So $R - r \approx 0.159155$ miles

to make sense of this result convert to feet

$$0.159155 \text{ miles} \left(\frac{5280 \text{ ft.}}{\text{mile}} \right) \quad \text{becomes}$$

(approx) 840.3384 ft

Second solution pathway for the Belt Problem.

$$\text{Using Variables}$$

$$\text{Let } C_E = \text{Circum of Earth}$$

$$C_B = \text{Circum of circle made by the belt suspended above the Earth}$$

$$\text{So the goal remain } R - r$$

$$\text{We have } C_B = 2\pi R \text{ and } C_E = 2\pi r$$

$$\text{It follows that } C_B - C_E = 1 \text{ mile (given)}$$

$$2\pi R - 2\pi r = 1 \text{ mile}$$

$$2\pi (R - r) = 1 \text{ mile}$$

$$\frac{2\pi(R-r)}{2\pi} = \frac{1 \text{ mile}}{2\pi}$$

$$\underline{\text{EXACT ANS.}} \qquad R - r = \frac{1}{2\pi} \text{ miles}$$

$$\text{conver } \frac{1}{2\pi} \text{ miles to feet}$$

$$\frac{1}{2\pi} \text{ miles} \left(\frac{5280 \text{ ft}}{\text{mile}} \right)$$

$$\text{so } \quad R - r \approx 840.3380995 \text{ feet}$$

What if we added L miles to the belt instead of just 1 mile? Tis second solution pathway allows the

solver to easily see that the result would be $\dfrac{L}{2p}$.

The Roof Problem

Two important skills are illustrated in this problem.   First, drawing auxiliary lines to make progress is a useful strategy. Second, as in real life, sketches are often NOT drawn to scale. Consequently, the problem solver must rely on the accuracy of her/his mathematical arguments rather than the appearance of a drawing.

Purpose: Draw auxiliary lines to make progress.

The Roof Problem (adapted from released Smarter Balanced Items, NSF, DC., 2013)
Given: The schematic drawing of a roof structure. Segments AG = 6 feet, CE = 12 feet,
GF = 2 feet, and   FE = 12 inches. Find the length of segment FB. Write any assumptions
you make and provide a thorough mathematical justification that will convince the
reader. Write your answer as a complete sentence. Note: The schematic may <u>not</u> be
accurately drawn to scale.

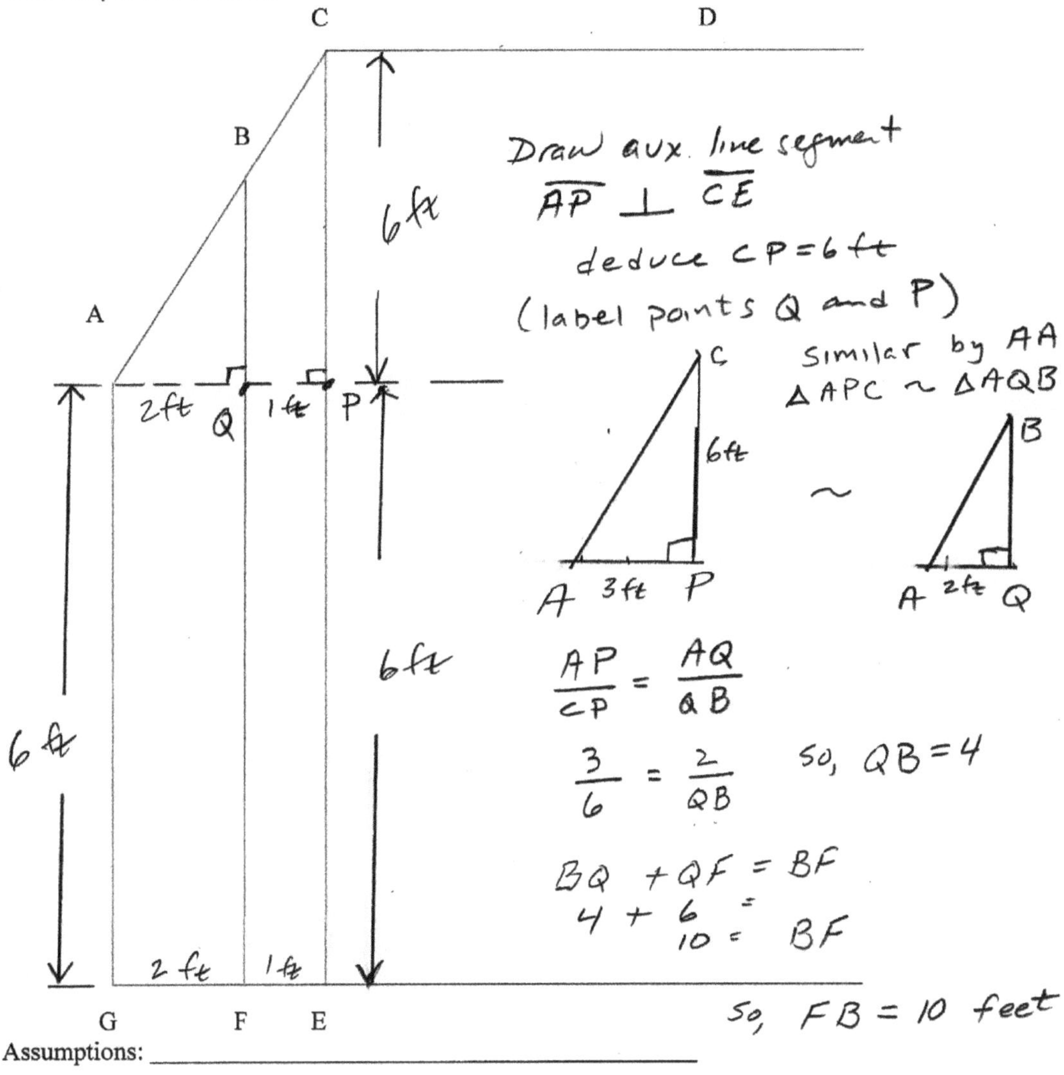

Assumptions: ____

The Kalamazoo Problem

You drive at a constant speed from Chicago to Detroit, a distance of 275 miles. About 120 miles from Chicago you pass through Kalamazoo, Michigan. Sketch a (labeled) graph of your distance from Kalamazoo as a function of time.

The key ideas in this problem are to recognize that the speed is *constant* but NOT given; and to label the vertical axis of the graph NOT as simply *"distance"* but rather *"**distance from Kalamazoo.**"*

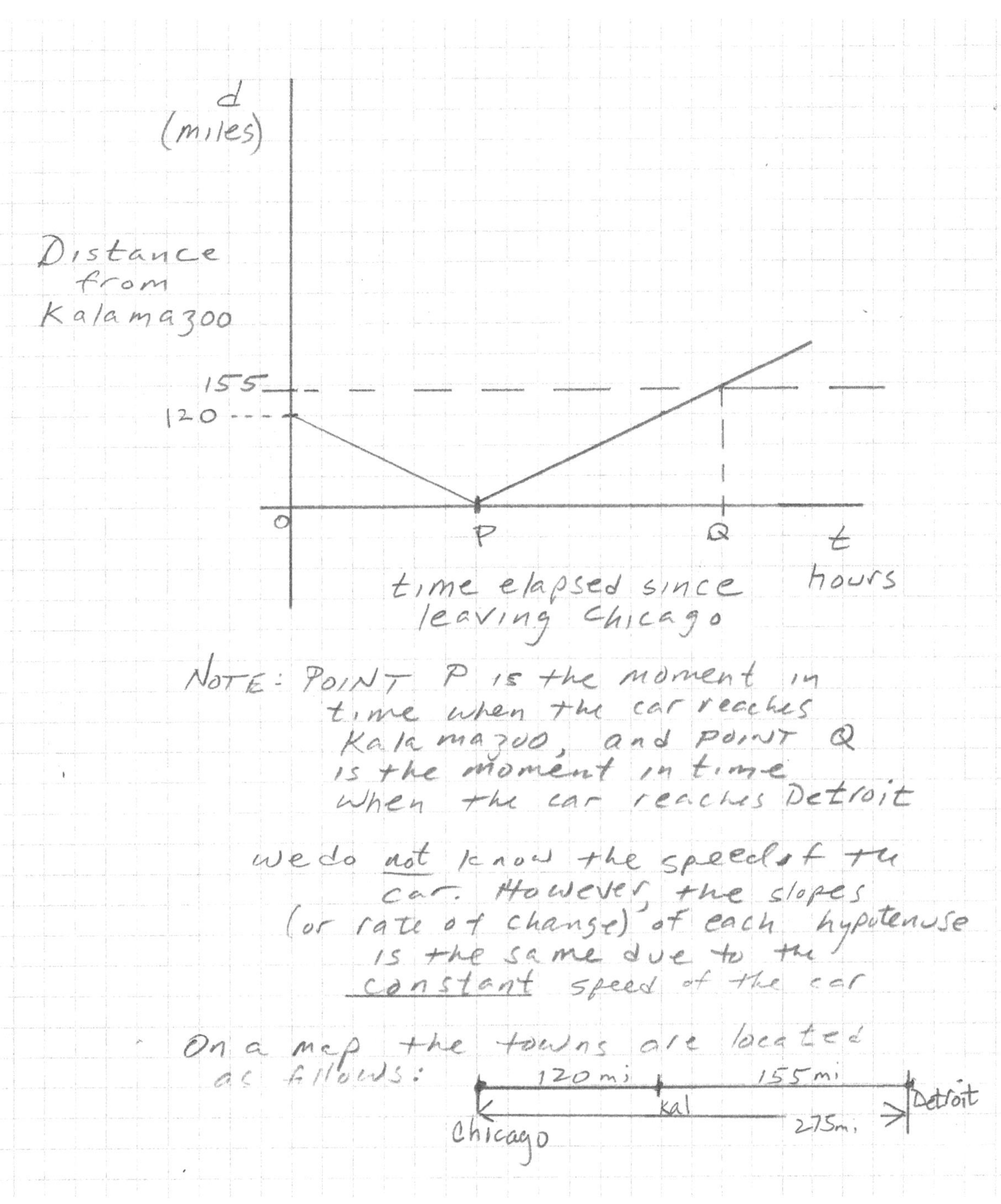

NOTE: POINT P is the moment in
time when the car reaches
Kalamazoo, and POINT Q
is the moment in time
when the car reaches Detroit

We do not know the speed of the
car. However, the slopes
(or rate of change) of each hypotenuse
is the same due to the
constant speed of the car

On a map the towns are located
as follows:

Requirements for Rigorous Graphs

Every graph should include the following labels to help the reader follow the solver's thinking and meaning: The meaning of ach axis, any significant coordinates, variables (case sensitive), and units of measure.

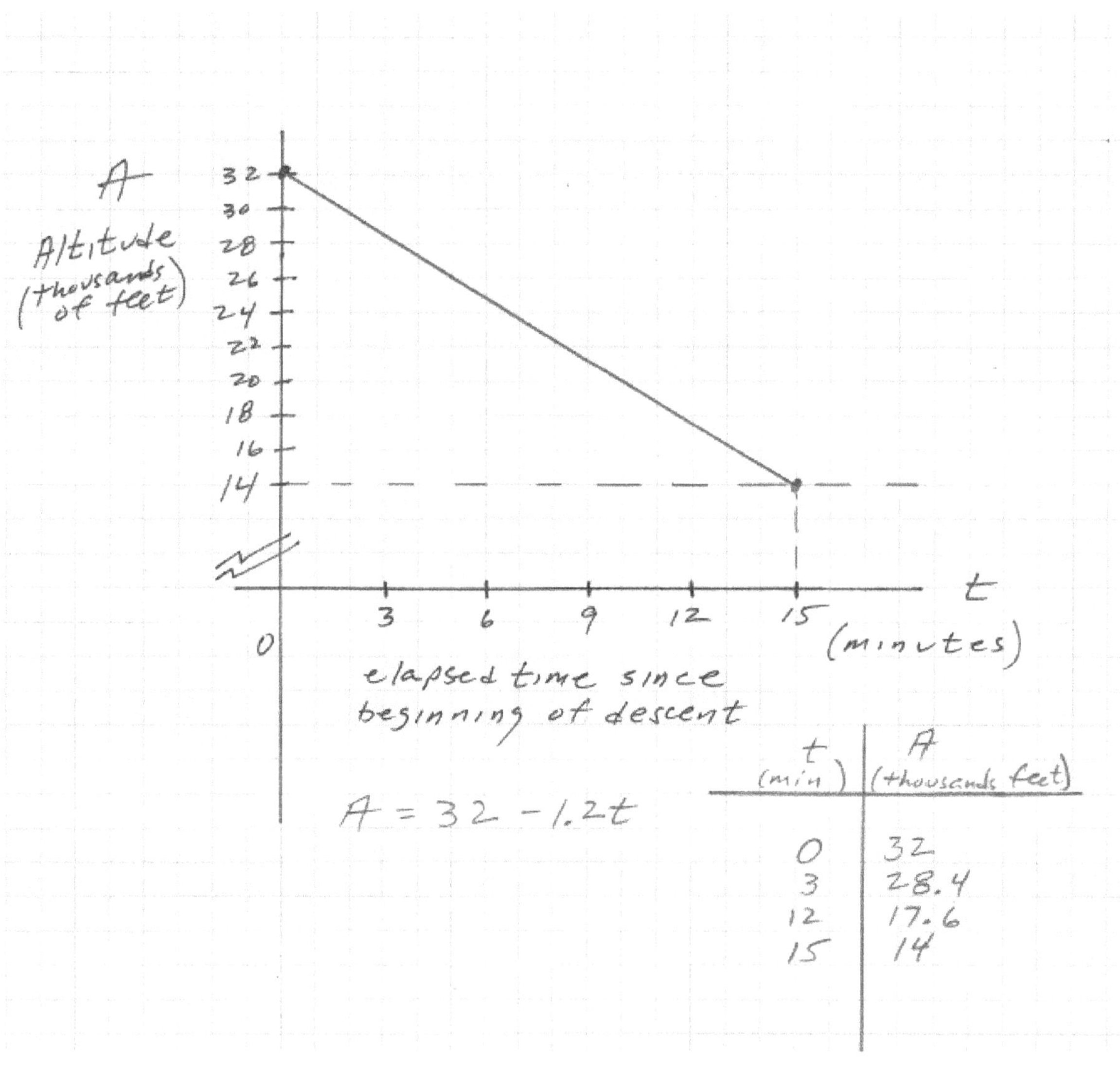

t (min)	A (thousands feet)
0	32
3	28.4
12	17.6
15	14

Recommended Resources

The gold standard in mathematics education for a resource is that it is grounded in research and peer-reviewed literature. Although there are many websites that offer problems and sheets of repetitive exercises there are few websites that offer well-designed program written by a collaboration of teachers and researchers. Two of the top websites that I recommend are:

NCTM (National Council of Teachers of Mathematics). Historically this is the prime organization that K-12 teachers have used over the decades in the United States. Although you can find free resources a paid membership is required to fully access all resources. I recommend buying an annual membership for in-service teachers, students, and parents. Journal publications keep you at the forefront of innovations in our field. Most importantly are the national standards and practices for teaching and learning mathematics. You will also find classroom resources, publications, research information, and conferences and professional development opportunities.
Begin exploring NCTM here: https://www.nctm.org/classroomresources/

YOUCUBED is a research-based program that is led by Dr. Jo Boaler from Stanford. The mission of the program "is to inspire, educate and empower teachers of mathematics, transforming the latest research on maths learning into accessible and practical forms." At the website, you will find tasks, videos, books, and more. Excellent for a teacher, homeschooler, or parent to use as a comprehensive guide to improve students' learning of mathematics. Many resources are free to download.

Begin with: *https://www.youcubed.org*, and then use *https://www.youcubed.org/resources/*

Additional Answers

The Ship Problem. Ships will pass each other on the open sea 102 times. A useful strategy is to find how many open sea crossings are NOT possible, 42, (this strategy is called finding the complement).

Use of Conjecture, Estimation, and Measurement. The length of the side of the square as described will be approximately 50.8 miles.

The Ma Study. The child's claim is false. One counterexample is a rectangle with sides (measured in inches) of 8, 0.5, 8, and 0.5 giving a perimeter of 17 inches but an area of 4 square inches.

Developing a Coherent mathematical Argument. L = S

Playground Problem. The pleasant surprise is that the new playground is four times as large as the original playground.

Focus on Mathematical Representation. The maximum area of the inscribed rectangle is 300 square feet and occurs when the base is 15 feet, and the height is 20 feet.

Resource Problem: Stack of Nickels. A stack of nickels that is 8 feet high contains 1,536 nickels and is worth $76.80

Resource Problem: Triangular Array. The number directly below 122 will be 146.

Resource Problem: Train Problem. It will take the train 15 minutes to completely pass through the tunnel while traveling at 12 miles per hour.

The Benton Problem. The area of the oblique rectangle is 2 square units.

A Lesson in Notation and deconstructing Complicated Figures.

Area of the field found by deconstructing a complicated figure. Draw and label the rectangle and two semi-circles separately. Note, all lineal measurements must use a common unit. Convert the perimeter to either yards or feet (standard for athletic fields in the USA).

Using yards, the total area of the field = $440r - \pi r^2$ *square yards*; or
Using feet, the total area of the field = $1320r - \pi r^2$ *square feet*.

The Border Problem. 10 by 10 has 36 shaded squares; 6 by 6 has 20 shaded squares; 15 by 15 has 56 shaded squares; 253 by 253 has 1008 shaded squares; and the n by n has $4n - 4$ shaded squares.

Follow-Up to the Border Problem. Total cost including the extra 5% will be $30,800

Matt Weber Problem. The area of the shaded right triangle is 6 square inches.

Ratio and Proportion in the real World. (top) The train was traveling at 48 miles per hour. (Bottom) The capacity of the gas tank is approximately 17 gallons.

Unpacking the Quadratic Formula. Rewrite the Quadratic Formula as $x = \dfrac{-b}{2a} \pm \dfrac{\sqrt{b^2 - 4ac}}{2a}$ Where the axis of symmetry of the parabola is a vertical line described by $x = \dfrac{-b}{2a}$ and the distance from the axis of symmetry to either root is given by $\dfrac{\sqrt{b^2 - 4ac}}{2a}$.

In this problem the axis of symmetry is given by x = 3 and the roots (or x-intercepts) are

$x = 3 - \sqrt{11}$ and $x = 3 + \sqrt{11}$.

Meaning and Sense-Making. The runway must be 4400 feet or $\dfrac{5}{6}$ of a mile.

Develop a Student's Curiosity. Yes, the claim can be ***proven*** to be true.

The Pipe Problem. It would take 256 pipes of diameter one-half inch to replace the capacity of a single eight-inch diameter pipe.

Optimization: Rancher Problem. The maximum area of 1,620,000 square feet occurs when the short side of the enclosed field is 900 feet and the side parallel to the river is 1,800 feet.

Note to my readers. You must develop confidence in your ability to verify that your answers make sense from both a practical point of view as well as from a mathematical point of view. Making errors is a natural part of doing mathematics but the best mathematicians are able to find their errors and correct the mistakes. Try to connect with other readers and develop a network of support to be able to share alternate solution pathways and your passion for problem solving.

www.ingramcontent.com/pod-product-compliance
Lightning Source LLC
Chambersburg PA
CBHW041833110726
48006CB00020B/2608